What others are sayi

Success and leaders
collection of these w
voices share collectively how there are many ways to climb, with God's help, to the top of the mountain. These women will encourage, equip, educate, inspire, and sometimes entertain you. Thank you, sweet sisters, for helping us all become all God-created us to be to do all created us to do.

—Pam Farrel, author of 58 books including *7 Simple Skills for Every Woman* **and bestselling** *Men Are Like Waffles, Women Are Like Spaghetti*

If you've been through some stuff that's made you feel torn down in purpose, this book is your bounce-back."

—Sharon Oliver, CEO and Founder of Creative Playground, Former publisher of CEO Magazine, Richmond, Virginia

Leadership is tough—especially when it comes upon us, unaware and even unsought. In *Leading Ladies: Discover Your God-Grown Strategies for Success*, authors Amber Weigand-Buckley and Lisa Burris Burns assemble a cast of leading ladies to encourage us, remind us of God's provision, and guide us down a well-traveled road. Truly a book for every woman to read and share with those she loves!

—Edie Melson, Director of the Blue Ridge Mountains Christian Writers Conference

I love the diversity of the voices in *Leading Ladies* as well as the unity of authentic hearts who are championing a generation of women to encourage and lift each other as we all move together to achieve even greater things.

—LeAnn Weiss-Rupard, president of Encouragement Company & bestselling *Hugs* **(trademark) author**

If you have dust-covered dreams, this book will help you rediscover and act on them. Throughout each chapter, you'll find opportunities for reflection and practical next steps to help you walk in all God has planned for you.

—Linda Morrison, NewYork Her Director, New York Ministry Network, Marketplace Chaplain, Leadership/Life Coach

Amber Weigand-Buckley
& Lisa Burris Burns
Leading Ladies
Discover Your God-Grown Strategy for Success
with
Candace Payne, Katy Nichole, GiGi Orsillo, Kerri Pomarolli,
Jane Jenkins Herlong, Veronica Clay, Kymberli Joye, Jacquelyn Marushka, Nancy Bogart,
Martha Bolton, Monica Schmelter, Erica Wiggenhorn & more
Foreword by Babbie Mason

Leading Ladies

Discover Your God-Grown Strategy for Success

Amber Weigand-Buckley
Lisa Burris Burns

Bold Vision Books
PO Box 2011
Friendswood, TX 77549

ISBN 978-1-946708-91-5
Library of Congress Control Number 2023938807

Published by Bold Vision Books, PO Box 2011, Friendswood, Texas 77549
www.boldvisionbooks.com

Edited by Cherry D. McGregor
Cover Design by Amber Weigand-Buckley, #barefacedcreativemedia
Interior design by kae Creative Solutions/#barefacedcreativemedia
Published in the United States of America.

DEDICATION

Amber–

For my husband Philip and my girls who gave me so much support and grace during this take-out season of our lives. Stuart and Stanley for the zen garden grooming moments which provided me with much needed stress relief. Also big love for my ride or die bestie Lisa who said "Yes" to jumping into the deep end yet again on this bigger-than-me project. You are a friend that loves closer than a sister.

Father, I take one step and you continue to multiply the work. Thank you for using me.

I am astounded beyond measure (Habakkuk 1:5).

Lisa–

Dedicated to my love Randy, the amazing humans we've parented whether by birth, marriage or borrowed, the sweetest Grandbabes, and my Mom and Daddy.

Amber, I can't imagine this journey without you. I am always ready for the next project or predicament we get into. Sister-Friends forever.

Heavenly Father, I say yes to new adventures. So long as you are with me, I'm in. My desire is to walk with you forever. (Psalms 23:6)

TABLE OF CONTENTS

FOREWORD

God is using His children like never before. In fact, He said He would do this in Acts 2:17,

> **"And it will be in the last days, says God, that I will pour out my Spirit on all flesh. Then your sons and your daughters will prophesy, your young men will see visions, and your old men will dream dreams" (NIV).**

God is calling and empowering you to proclaim your faith in Christ boldly, without apology. He is asking you to teach and encourage others to do the same. He is raising up a generation of world-changing women excited about furthering the Good News of the saving grace of Jesus Christ in every way, to everyone, in every place.

Do you know the reason you were created? You are created to make God look good through the work you do here on Earth. God stores gifts in our hearts and brings all the good stuff to the table—our sensitivity, compassion, and love. We can use those gifts to shine light in this dark and needy world. When we turn the light up, we shine so much brighter. Compassion will flow. Love will change and touch hearts. We will see the result as we let our light so shine before men that they may see our good works and glorify our Father. (See Matthew 5:16)

Do we have it all together? Certainly not. Do we know the God who holds it all together on the good days or when life is unraveling at the seams? Absolutely. This book, ***Leading Ladies***, is a must-read. Behind every one of these amazing stories is a victorious daughter of the Most-High King, who hopes to lift you up above your circumstances.

As you sit down with this book, by faith, you are pulling up a seat to join a united circle of sisters in the Lord. Representing all ages, hues, backgrounds, and job descriptions, so you can become a part of this community of ***Leading Ladies***—we all have the same job to do.

Whenever I read a book that resonates deeply with my experience, I recommend it to others. This book will encourage and motivate you to acknowledge and walk in God's greater purposes.

Babbie Mason
Singer-songwriter, author, and speaker
Babbie.com
BabbieMasonRadio.com

Introduction

This book began with a question.

As I sat waiting in the carline to pick my youngest daughter up after school one afternoon I heard it, and dare I say felt it, all at the same time.

"Do you recognize the gifts I've placed within you—and how I've equipped *you* to lead?"

Immediately there was a disconnect—I felt frozen. Me, a leader? I don't lead. I'm an advice giver.

Although my desire has always been to come alongside and encourage women, helping them to embrace and walk in their talents, I wasn't connecting that to my own ability to make an impact and be an actual leader. My mental health label, along with the daily grind of life, had clouded my self-worth. In the days following, I came to realize I equated my life to checking off daily task lists for everybody else. Working through God's carline question brought new awareness and realization. Maybe the Father wanted to change my perspective about who I am and what He had me here to do.

Romans 4:17 is a scripture I had been drawn to for quite some time, and now it was making such perfect sense.

> "We call Abraham 'father' not because he got God's attention by living like a saint, but because God made something out of Abraham when he was a nobody. Isn't that what we've always read in Scripture, God saying to Abraham, 'I set you up as father of many peoples'? Abraham was first named 'father'

> and then became a father because he dared to trust God to do what only God could do: raise the dead to life, with a word make something out of nothing. When everything was hopeless, Abraham believed anyway, deciding to live not on the basis of what he saw he couldn't do but on what God said he would do" (The Message).

When everything seems hopeless, believe anyway. I had to choose to live based upon who God said I was and not what I accomplished. It's been an ongoing journey (almost a half century), but I believe I'm starting to catch a glimpse of who that woman is, and I truly believe God wants to help you do the same for yourself.

Lisa and I are so excited to introduce you to more than 30 world-changing women—all hues, all backgrounds, all walks of life—famous to not-so-famous. We hope they will inspire you to dig deep and connect with the goodness God has placed within you.

—Amber

Lead Me On

I will follow you into the unknown,
Where my eyes have not seen and my feet have not gone.
For this path it is narrow and easy to stray.
In grace will you keep me and show me the way?

Oh lead me, Lead me on.
And I'll be your vessel in the great unknown.
And I will borrow your peace in the midst of the storm.
For the stars they are dimmest in moments of doubt.
Lord be the compass that steadies the path,
And leads me, Leads me on.

I've found more in the risk of surrender, than the comforts of home.
I have peace in the moments of chaos knowing you hold it all.
I've found more in the winds of your testing than the safety of shores.
I have joy in the moments of suffering, knowing morning will come.

So lead me on. Lead me on
To the great unknown, lead me on
So lead me on, Oh lead me on.
Oh I'm ready now. Lead me on.

I'll carry your promise into the unknown,
For your word is a fountain that quenches my soul.
And I will trust in the desert and wait for the rain.
I know that rivers will flow once again and lead me,
they'll lead me on.

Lyrics and Music by Michaelah Weaver for LeadingLadies.Life. Copyright 2023.

Michaelah is an award-winning singer-songwriter and worship leader (Abundant Life, Lee's Summit, Missouri). She's a member of The Keepers Co. with husband Kaleb. They are parents of three girls.

CHAPTER 1

Take Off the Makeup

Amber Weigand-Buckley

Multi-award-winning editor and art director of *Leading Hearts* magazine Amber Weigand-Buckley (barefacedgirl.com) faces mental health challenges daily with a hefty dose of self-awareness, self-care, professional psychiatric guidance, and medication, reinforced with pit-bull perseverance and a lot of Jesus-filled grace.

However, she never dreamed a severe bipolar episode and the walk from shame to authentic healing would open the door for God to grow her in leadership—beyond what she could have imagined. As the owner of #barefacedcreativemedia and marketing director for the Advanced Writers and Speakers Association, Amber has the privilege of helping world-changing women find their wings, hone their skills, and take their God-calling to the next level.

"Hi, my name is Amber. I'm a bipolar woman, and I am a leader." Sometimes when I say those words, I feel like I just arrived at my first AA meeting.

I'm not a healed bipolar or a recovered bipolar. I take medication daily and navigate life differently. My family knows bipolar disorder is a part of my DNA. But I still have faith, and I still believe in miracles. I love God, and I love that I'm one of many, just like you, called to lead uniquely. It took me a while to feel qualified to lead again, but it wasn't because God magically changed my brain chemistry. It came in knowing God uses all my divinely created beauty and steps into my weaknesses so I might lead others to a fuller knowledge of him.

I'm part of a sisterhood. I'd call it a humankind-hood. Like many on this round planet, I face the challenge of keeping life focused while battling a bunch of brain activity that doesn't like to play nice. Sometimes my thoughts move so fast it's hard to tie them down, and I get depressed or anxiety ridden when I can't keep up. If I can do anything with my journey, it's giving the world a greater understanding of what the face of mental illness looks like and how it looks a lot like me. It took a long time for me to realize that this condition does not disqualify me from God's leadership call on my life.

Going Barefaced

I didn't realize I was having a breakdown when it happened. On the surface, I was 38, an editor for an award-winning Christian youth magazine, a credentialed minister with the same organization I worked for, and a quirky, flower-child creative who wanted to challenge teens and stretch the Church. Down deeper, I had secrets. A childhood with a don't talk about the abusive atmosphere in your home, or your dad might lose his job in his Christian workplace dynamic. I couldn't believe that in adulthood I'd let the dysfunctional home life I left behind seep into 19 years of marriage with similarly toxic patterns.

Writing was my therapy. Call me hypocritical, but some articles I wrote were, in reality, me talking to myself in the pit—working out what I knew was wrong, but trying to maintain the appearance needed to stay in a circle of leadership. After all, it seemed a sin to know something was wrong in private and not do anything about it publicly.

I desperately wanted change. I wanted to rip off the mask and find deep healing. As I tried to cope by seeking God and counsel, everything in my brain became an open fire hydrant. My writing, self-therapy, and journaling soon turned into six months when words wouldn't stop invading my sleep. At all times, I had a pen in my possession. I would write on anything I could get my hands on, even my own body. I spent my nights writing, my afternoons writing, and I would pull into parking lots and write. I was even exhausting my toilet-time writing. At the time, I saw something quite beautiful in those moments. It was a time of stripping off my makeup to deal with the real dirt of my humanity. It felt like God's grace and love shed light on who I was—a barefaced girl. Even now, I wonder, Is this how Edgar Allan Poe or Emily Dickinson descended into madness? Everything meant something just for me, and the rest of the world was just clueless.

Some moments seemed euphoric and beautiful, while others were the darkest feelings I'd ever experienced. My writings unraveled light, goodness, and darkness until it became a tangled knot. I let people into my headspace who never should have been there. I was disillusioned into thinking I could never make life right. The darkness, regret, and hopelessness were so thick, I didn't think I would ever find good again. Or that I ever would have the possibility of being more than damaged goods, meaning I was unfit for ministry. Before anyone could find out what was truly going on inside my head, I let go of my ministerial license—I was unfit to hold any called by God titles.

The pit got darker, and then the enemy handed me a shovel while I was down there. I made choices I told myself I would never make—choices I thought were justifiable. I would volley between anger and wanting to make situations right. I apologized repeatedly to God, wanting the feelings I stumbled over and my destructive behavior to be removed from me. All the while, my husband was doing everything he could for all the right reasons—allowing his own character to be revealed in repentance and seeking to care for me. Frankly, I just wanted him to pay for my pain and I wanted to give him a reason to walk away. But God, in his redemptive nature, had a different plan. He allowed the one who hurt me the most deeply to bring comfort and quiet to my head when all I could feel was lonely and dark.

Pause and Reflect

What are some secrets that may be holding you hostage? How have you sought to deal with them? Who are your most trusted friends, the ones you can confide in on your journey to deep healing? Have you considered the need for professional intervention? Why or why not?

From the Edge

I remember the day that darkness tried to put a stake in my head. I had just finished teaching a room full of Christian writers about creatively reaching the millennial generation with a gospel that sticks. An hour later, I stood alone on the edge of a mountain in Colorado. A voice speaking from the darkness I had been internalizing said, "If your life matters, if the good outweighs the shadows in your soul, God will save you if you step off this cliff." I remember contemplating, looking at the space in front of my toes and then down hundreds of feet. In those moments, a familiar and loving voice broke through. "Daughter, you need to recognize my voice and turn around." And I stepped back.

All along this path, God was knocking on my door. He was doing everything he could to pursue me, and he would never let this injured sheep go without a fight. Months following this episode, I experienced prolonged physical illness in my body, coupled with seeing and hearing things that weren't there. Extreme emotional highs one moment, swinging to exhausting lows the next. It was like every emotion in my body was attacking me at once—even the good ones.

My husband and I, fortunately, had an appointment with our counselor. It was then I decided to take the counselor's advice and go to the hospital. In the back of my mind, I believed professionals at the hospital would prove me to be rational. That time behind a psychiatric ward door would end up being my biggest blessing in disguise. It was like God pushed a divine pause button in my life.

Pause and Reflect

Recall a time regarding unresolved hurt when God brought your life to a pause. What are some of the greatest hurdles with which you've dealt? How can you be proactive in keeping your personal, mental, relational, and spiritual health in focus?

Surviving My Head-in Collision

When my brain broke, I thought it was the end. My life as a writer and leader for Christ was over. It was hard to speak, and I barely had the presence of mind to drive. I had a massive head injury and I never thought I'd ever put a sentence together again. I would physically touch my skull to reassure myself that my brains weren't visible through my hair. My husband and daughters were patient and picked up the slack as if I was recovering from a massive car accident. God took the time to help me recover from this tsunami that slammed my life. It took almost a year before I fully recovered my ability to write.

The "B-Word" [bahy-poh-ler]

I'm not going to lie. When I received my diagnosis of Bipolar Type 2 with psychotic episodes, I felt as if someone handed me a cone of shame. As a leader, I was ashamed I had come unglued in front of people I loved, desired respect from, and had the responsibility to encourage. I was supposed to be a role model, leading others to the goodness of God. I wallowed in the toxic mess of my mind and allowed negative influencers to justify and affirm my unhealthy shift.

Although the pit diagnosis seemed to be a life sentence, with time, I learned it wasn't my God-ordained dwelling place. It was time to give up the cone of shame. It was time to be barefaced, honest, and transparent concerning my condition. God wanted to use my voice to dissolve the stigma of the b-word.

Pause and Reflect

Are there situations you've dealt with secretly in the past, or are walking through currently? Do you feel it disqualifies you for leadership? What intentional steps can you take to find true freedom and honesty as a leader?

We Walk, But We Never Walk Alone

I walk this journey with stigma and stereotypes. I've learned if I want to be transparent about what I have walked through, I must learn to be comfortable with those who are uncomfortable with my vulnerability.

Every day I wonder at the scars and symptoms—black holes of memory loss from that time. I believe it's the grace of God. You don't need reminding of what you've done. Yes, I take medicine to relieve symptoms. But God certainly knows I never want to be toxically sick again.

I had to realize my call to lead—all the good, the bad, the ugly, and everything in between—is crowned with vision from Genesis 50:20. "You intended to harm me, but God intended it for good to accomplish what is now being done, the saving of many lives" (NIV).

I haven't seen a rainbow of promise that I will never relapse. I know it could happen. But if it does, I pray the Church will be gracious, just like my Savior who dishes grace lavishly on my Spirit-breathed dirt and bones. And even if it should happen again, my rainbow of promise is that God will always walk with me. He is present even in our crazy, and he hangs out in our pits of personal despair.

I've realized as a leader that my hedge of influencers must be women who speak life into me for the good of my spirit. Not everyone needs to know your deepest failures or details. You just need a select few on your ride-or-die team. And if you haven't found them yet, I can guarantee your walking through shame, hurt, and pain will quickly reveal your genuine friends.

This path of brokenness has taught me a powerful truth—striving for perfection does not serve me. Covering up my flawed dirt does not strengthen me. I've not come here to build flimsy, out-of-reach polished platforms. I'm a 2 Corinthians 12:9 influencer.

"My grace is sufficient for you, for my power is made perfect in weakness. Therefore, I will boast all the more gladly about my weaknesses, so that Christ's power may rest on me" (NIV).

In this journey, as with any illness, I've also learned you can't traverse it with your own determination to be well. In fact, the healthiest action you can take is to step back from shame and realize you need help. Without help, the darkness only becomes darker and more powerful. No matter who you are or what position of influence you hold, there is great freedom in simply taking a deep breath and courageously stepping forward to find healing. It takes getting to this place to deal more efficiently with day-to-day challenges.

Personally, it's amazing to see the richness God has revealed through my journey. Writing is not simply something I do. Now, I've learned to write from a place of vulnerability which has been pressed from the depth of who I am.

This journey has taken me from smoke-and-mirrors prestige to a place of barefaced influence, and for that I am grateful. I am actively praying for those of you who deal with mental health struggles. I ask God to allow you to know that he has called you to lead—you have something beautifully unique to give the world for his glory.

Leading in Prayer

Heavenly Father, thank you for taking all that we have—even what the world says is broken and useless—and repurposing it for your glory. Help me lay everything at your feet, especially things that appear shameful. Help me realize I don't need to carry them alone secretly. Take away the fear of judgment, empowering me to reach out and experience freedom in your restoring power. Help me learn to love myself the way you love me and wear the mantle of leadership in the way you've uniquely designed for me. Amen.

"My brokenness is a better bridge for people than my pretend wholeness ever was."

-Sheila Walsh

Recording Artist,
Evangelist
& Television Host

CHAPTER 2

Stop Waiting for Permission

Tracy Glass

When you are called to lead, it's tempting to wait to get off the bench until someone "needs you." Tracy Glass, who leads as a life coach, Bible teacher, and author, has a message for you. "Girl, get up and do what God is calling you to do."

As an influencer in the church arena, Tracy experienced her ground zero when she walked through the heartache and shame of divorce and transitioned to single motherhood. She now utilizes her fiery insight to inspire hurting women to step into their God-created purpose.

Can I? May I? Please. These are common permission words. Where did we learn to ask before we act? Did the lesson come from our parents when they told us to be seen and not heard? Or was it our grade school teachers who taught us to raise our hands before speaking?

Possibly, asking permission before we say and do comes from the feeling we need the approval of others. It could also be because we desire to fit into a people group or club to be accepted. The club has rules, a code of conduct, and compliance expectations, silently convincing us to pursue their goals and dreams. Our dreams and goals sit in a corner, accumulating dust and asking us, "When are you going to pick us up again?"

I learned from childhood that my role was to serve others. My mother taught me the true definition of joy meant putting Jesus first, others second, and yourself last. This definition of joy sounds good, but I noticed I was too depleted to serve myself after I served in ministry and served my family. So, what was I doing wrong?

I come from a family of superhero women. My mother is eighty years old. She has a fantastic talent for giving, supporting, and loving everyone she calls her family or friend. Recently, we were having a conversation, and I told her about a New Year's goal.

"Mom, this year, I need to learn how to establish better boundaries with others. I feel I'm giving a lot, but I'm not getting much back." Her response surprised me.

"Do you feel I taught you to put everyone else first?"

My response to her was, "Yes."

There is nothing wrong with putting others first. The problem arises when we put others and our plans before what God asks us to do.

Pause and Reflect

Do you have a dream on hold because you are currently putting another person or their project before your God-given assignment? What would it take to step into your dream today?

Get Unleashed to Go

Someone once told me, "You just need to sit there and look pretty." In other words, I don't want to hear what you have to say because what you have to say isn't necessary. When others don't listen to what we have to say, invalidate our opinions, don't engage us, or do not invite us to have a seat at the table, we can feel small. Our greatness—creativity, boldness, and dreams—can go into hiding in those moments.

There was a season in my life when I had a skewed perspective on who God had called me to be. I was hiding because I carried a secret rule in my heart—don't shine too brightly, Tracy. Don't draw attention to yourself because you don't want to come across as prideful. However, this personal and internal view I held was challenged when a friend asked me a powerful question.

"It feels like you hold back in telling your story. Why?" She made me question myself on a deeper level. Was I holding back because of pride or shame?

Wow. I didn't realize I was holding back, especially concerning my life being restored after a painful divorce. I discovered I needed to learn how to share my complete restoration story boldly and not hold back anything—the good, bad, and ugly parts, too. The women within our circles of influence are often hurting and want to heal desperately. We must authentically share our challenges and triumphs to be relatable and effective in leading.

God constantly reminds me to tell the complete story of my life, not just the saved and set-free version. Bold leadership is when we can share our testimonies, even if they revoke our club membership. Others are set free when we lead boldly and tell the truth about our story.

Revelation 12:11 reminds us, "They conquered him completely through the blood of the Lamb and the powerful word of his testimony. They triumphed because they did not love and cling to their own lives, even when faced with death" (TPT).

Pause and Reflect

How is God guiding you to influence others? Evaluate your complete story, even the parts you would rather not talk about. How can God use those moments to reach others?

The Risk of Not Leading Boldly

For those prone to be pleasers, coloring within the lines is where we thrive. We feel safe within boundaries because veering too much to the left or right is risky. Who wants to be judged, reprimanded, or exposed?

The problem with coloring solely within lines is that we risk living unfulfilled lives. We hold back from fully pursuing our God-created purpose. He desires us to become bold and bodacious women who flow according to his Word and not the world's code of conduct. The only code we follow is what Jesus told us to do in Matthew 28:18-20, which states Jesus' instructions and commission, or what I like to call our go.

"Then Jesus came close to them and said, 'All authority of the universe has been given to me. Now wherever you go, make disciples of all nations, baptizing them in the name of the Father, the Son, and the Holy Spirit. And teach them to faithfully follow all that I have commanded you. And never forget that I am with you every day, even to the completion of this age'" (TPT).

In this scripture, Jesus delegated authority to his disciples to go, run, and tell the world the Good News.

To share what Jesus offers others—salvation, eternal life, abundant and victorious living.

The disciples didn't delay or hold back. Instead, they moved forward with passion and zeal to accomplish what Jesus told them to do. But they were afraid. I'm sure they didn't feel qualified. They probably wondered if they could do anything without Jesus in the flesh. Jesus knew they would have these emotions because his last words before his ascension were, "And never forget that I am with you every day, even to the completion of this age" (Matthew 28:20 TPT).

Pause and Reflect

What boundaries or limitations do you believe keep you from being used by God? Can you allow yourself to envision your personal ***go***? Ask God to help you list ways to expand and shift your vision and direction.

Be Bold Even When it's Uncomfortable

Imagine for a moment you and Jesus are having a conversation, and he says, "Why did you let fear hold you captive and prevent you from stepping out in my power and commission?"

For many of us, fear is the door keeping us locked away. Fear from potential disapproval keeps us frozen. Fear quickly leads to shame and guilt. The enemy's voice can whisper how unqualified we are because we are still dealing with the after-effects of our own battles. We conclude it's too risky to lead at this time. We certainly can't lead in transparent honesty, risking our secret issues to exposure. The loud voice of condemnation stops us in our tracks.

When we feel frozen, we need to picture Jesus. He is in front of us, cheering us on to overcome our fears, insecurities, and limitations. He invites us to take his hand as we stretch beyond our uncomfortable and uncontrollable places. When fear causes me to go into hiding, I've discovered I feel empty, frustrated, and disappointed.

As I coach and mentor women, they occasionally express something is missing. They feel dissatisfaction, frustration, and even anger. Why? It often points back to this question, "Are we fulfilling the customized commission God has called us to do, the way He called us to do it, without shrinking back?" Often, the root of our frustration is because we are leading off-course. God asks us to veer right, but we insist on going left.

You Have His Permission to Shine Bright

God is compelling us to lead boldly with a fresh perspective—with Jesus-perspective. His goal is to fulfill the will of his father. So, let's not allow the invisible leash of our insecurities, bias, past, fears, negative self-talk, or anything else to hold us back from taking bold steps of faith.

What is bold leadership? It's doing what God has asked us to do fully. It's asking others to follow us only as we follow Christ. The best leadership is when our goal mirrors Christ's mission to serve others. Everything we do points to Jesus—not building our popularity or social media following, not increasing our bank account, promoting our products or agenda.

Dr. Martin Luther King Jr. said, "But recognize that he who is greatest among you shall be your servant. That's a new definition of greatness. By defining greatness, everybody can be great because everybody can serve. You don't have to have a college degree to serve. You don't have to make your subject and verbs agree to serve. You only need a heart full of grace, a soul generated by love."

Let's not hold back in declaring why we are leaders—to lead others to the person who is leading us, Jesus.

Mark 10:45 says, "For even the Son of Man did not come to be served, but to serve, and to give his life as a ransom for many" (NIV).

Pause and Reflect

Are there any uncomfortable or impossible circumstances hindering you from stretching and taking bold steps in your God assignments? How are you serving and affirming others in fulfilling their God-created call and destiny?

Leading in Prayer

Heavenly Father, I acknowledge I have allowed pleasing others to override the importance of doing the work you have called me to do. Extract this mentality from my mind daily. I do not look to others to affirm where you are leading me. I will walk obediently, in tune with your Word and Spirit. Help me embrace your leadership call wherever I find my feet today. Amen.

"My mother did not raise me to ask for permission to lead."

-Ayanna Pressley

U.S. Congresswoman &
the first Black woman elected
to the Boston City Council

CHAPTER 3

FIND WHAT MAKES YOU SPARKLE

Jane Jenkins Herlong

Jane Jenkins Herlong is a Sirius XM Southern Humorist, award-winning speaker, professional singer, and recording artist. Jane was recently inducted into the prestigious Speaker Hall of Fame and is the author of five internationally best-selling/award-winning books.

A Southern farm girl, Jane walked through her family's tomato fields straight to the runway of the Miss America Pageant. Today, she shares her sweet tea wisdom and Southern-fried humor in her most recent *Sweet Tea Secrets from the Deep-Fried South* release

Yes, I am a pageant girl—big hair, over-the-top jewelry, sparkly gowns, etc. But please don't confuse me with Honey Boo Boo. To help discourage any judgments you might have regarding pageants and beauty queens, I want to share what I learned and how I have used these skills as a writer and speaker.

Pageant competition was all I had. I was not an athlete, nor was I a scholar. Raised on a vegetable farm in an old tenant house my father renovated, my daddy had a 10th-grade education and we struggled financially. However, I was a dreamer, with a vivid imagination, a sense of humor, and a desire to work hard. I believed anything was possible. Thankfully, through the pageant competition, I could attend graduate school with the scholarship money I won. Soon, I discovered my gifts, talent, and purpose. My first experience was my high school pageant competition for Miss Freshman.

I worked on my poise, wardrobe, and smile. I also learned to project confidence on a stage. Can you believe I was even crowned Miss South Carolina and competed in the Miss America Pageant? It's true.

As a professional speaker, I confidently walk when I step on the stage. I wear a complementary outfit and project joy. Can we all agree this is an essential asset in speaking? What I like about the whole pageant world is its giant self-improvement platform. I am constantly challenging myself to self-improve. I have a keynote entitled "You Can't Put High Heels on a Holstein."

Competition is good for your growth, stretching your abilities, and finding your purpose. Everything I learned from the four phases of competition as a contestant in the Miss America Pageant can help anyone move forward in their calling.

In a nutshell, these are the four purpose-building life skills:

- ☐ Be a good communicator
- ☐ Have a sense of personal style
- ☐ Take care of yourself physically
- ☐ Develop your talent

We can't get caught up thinking we must be the CEO of some big company to lead others. It's time to reframe ourselves in the unique gifts and influence God gives us in this life. We all have what we need to invest in others and give him glory. We all have these gifts—no one gets left out. This farm girl always had big dreams. But how do we use our talents? I encourage people to be brave and bold and find fun in any situation. Humor is healing. I love helping others tap into the best version of themselves. Figure out how you can encourage people you encounter. Maybe a person you meet has the personality of a younger version of yourself. You think, Been there, done that. Reach out. Sometimes we walk through seasons to bring strength to others just starting. Those are moments of influence that can't be taken for granted.

Pause and Reflect

Look back over your life and write down what you have learned, participated in, and accomplished that helped to springboard you into the woman you are today.

Talent ... What is Talent?

I define talent as whatever you can give back to serve others. That's it. My Aunt Naomi Herlong could bake a caramel cake like no other. She never used an electric beater; the consistency of using a large spoon was her guide when the cake was ready to bake. Growing up, our small community had an annual Grange competition, where the local farming community would all come together in their area of expertise. One way to receive points was cooking, and the community sure knew who to ask to share their culinary skills, my Aunt Naomi.

When the competition was over, the winner was, you guessed it, my community, Harmony. Today the Harmony Grange still stands. Although the Grange Society no longer exists, this modest building is now our Harmony Church Fellowship Hall. No talent is ever too small.

Writing is an integral part of speaking. My friend Larry Winget says, "If you have a speech, you have a book. If you have a book, you have a speech." I have always heard that you write if you want to be a good writer. The same goes for singing, speaking, etc.

So how did my talent and purpose meet up? It began with competition, and I also learned how to have a good sense of humor. The stakes get higher during the interview portion of the competition. Interview and excellent communication skills are vital both on and off the stage. I studied communication skills and how to express myself with clarity through stories, humor, motivation, and inspiration. Of course, growing up in the south—my family and friends were a source of great material. I loved doing voices.

If you know your gift but are struggling with how to use it, I'd like to encourage you to do a few things:

1. **Talk to the people that know you best. Ask them what they think you're good at doing. Often, we are already using our gift, and we don't even know it.**

2. **Think about what makes you happy. We gravitate to ways we can use our talents.**

3. **Pray. Ask God to reveal ways you can use your gift. Ask him to open doors that will grow your faith and build confidence.**

Pause and Reflect

Considering the three tips given above, how can you more effectively use the giftings you have to activate your purpose?

Boost That Confidence Level

And now, for everyone's favorite—the swimsuit competition. You are kidding—walk across the stage wearing a swimsuit, high heels, and a smile? I feared this part of the competition the most, and rightly so. When I was in graduate school, my professor asked me, "What is your worst phase of competition?"

"Swimsuit," I boldly declared.

"Well," continued my wise professor. "Wear your swimsuit under your clothes, and then it becomes part of you and your comfort zone." Point taken. So, I hit the stage with his advice, invested in a gym membership, and gained new confidence.

Pause and Reflect

Are there areas of your life that continually bump up against your comfort zone? How can you challenge yourself to push past uncomfortable roadblocks?

Face Your Fears to Find Your Purpose

Another critical element to finding your gifts and purpose is challenging yourself to face your fears. I lean on these two verses every single day. First, "God has not given us a spirit of fear but of power, and of love and of a sound mind" (2 Timothy 1:7 NKJV). Did you know Timothy struggled with being timid? Second, when I wake up in the morning, I always tell myself, "This is the day the Lord has made; I'm going to rejoice and be glad..." (See Psalm 118:24). Every day is a gift, so, I start my day with those two scriptures. Then I have quiet time or watch a television evangelist, and that sets the tone for the day.

Pause and Reflect

Commit to memorizing two scriptures that will set the tone for your day.

Use Your Life Lessons to Teach Others in Love

A true leader should be someone who speaks the truth in love, getting to the heart of the issue. When people need to learn life lessons, they look to people to teach them. If you've been down a dark road and survived, you have the knowledge and know-how to lead others. Now it's your turn to help someone else on their dark highway. The gift of helping is a spiritual gift. When we realize God has brought us down a similar road, we can use our experience to help others. That is a gift.

Pause and Reflect

What situation have you walked through, and gained experience from, that will help others navigate the same path? List three insights from this particular part of your journey.

Get Comfortable Being Uncomfortable

To the woman who feels they are floundering and not landing on purpose, get uncomfortable. Don't stay on the safe side. Step out of your comfort zone and do something different. I always say, "You don't know who you are until you have become who you think you are." Challenge yourself, and you will see a new you start to evolve. While writing *Sweet Tea Secrets from the Deep-Fried South*, I got a call from the United Talent Agency wanting to know about a screenplay. So, now I'm writing a script. And you know what? In school, I got an F in writing. My English professor copied my paper and said to the class, "Don't ever do this." Fast forward to when I spoke at my college's convocation. The professor who gave that F was in the audience. I handed him my book, now sold in Cracker Barrel stores.

So, the bottom line is to not let anybody define who you are. To discover your purpose, you've got to dive deep and find it. Then, show it off because that's the point of having talent. The final step is once you find it, use it to serve others.

Pause and Reflect

Has a perceived failure created a roadblock preventing you from walking in the fullness of your gifts? What steps can you take to revisit that gift and walk in it again?

Leading in Prayer

Heavenly Father, help me discover and delight in the talents you are growing in me. Grant me courage to carry out the plans you have for my life. As I step out of my comfort zone and into my destiny, let my gifts be a testimony to your goodness always. Amen.

"True confidence isn't about having an attitude of self-reliance or self-assurance. It comes from acknowledging that there is purpose where God has you in life right now. It's also in your obedience to trust Him and move you forward in life every step of the way."

-Tosca Lee

NY Times Bestselling Author, Former Mrs. Nebraska America (1996)/United States (1998) & First Runner-Up Mrs. United States

CHAPTER 4

Stop Striving for Perfection

Erica Wiggenhorn

Erica Wiggenhorn grew up in a home where success equated to a single word—perfection—an impossible bar to meet. She spent years striving to get as close as possible, only to feel defeated. After years in *performance prison* she realized the mark she ran so hard to hit was never her idea of success at all. It was passed down to her by her family. After a clear invitation from Christ to become part of his family, she is learning to rest in the sufficiency of grace.

As an influencer, award-winning author, and inspirational speaker, Erica wants to challenge you and weary women everywhere to stop striving for an elusive bar of success.

Growing up, I never could pinpoint what I wanted to do or be as an adult. My friends dreamed of being ballerinas, ice skaters, doctors, or hairstylists, but I never found anything particularly appealing. I now realize why. I could not envision myself being successful at it. And if I didn't know how to do it perfectly, or at least learn how to master it perfectly, I preferred to steer myself toward other pursuits where achieving perfection seemed possible. I had adopted my family's definition of success: If you couldn't reach the stars, you either needed to go in another direction or find a ladder to climb because only the height of stardom equated to worthiness.

I remember telling my father once that maybe I should be a teacher like my mother. He looked at me squarely and asked, "Why would you want to be a teacher? How about you start your own school?" In his eyes, being like everybody else was beneath me, and I should hatch bigger dreams. At that moment, I felt like my dad thought I could do anything. I also remember thinking, My dad doesn't know how terrifying that high expectation feels to me. I realized I would not be successful in his eyes unless I did something huge.

Imagine a relay runner in a track meet. Poised and positioned, waiting to take the baton, their hand remains outstretched behind them while they keep their eyes focused ahead. Their ears acutely attune to their teammate's approach from behind. They begin to run until they feel the metal rod in the palm of their hand. But they need to do more than feel it; they need to sense its perfect position to tighten their grip without dropping it. They must fully embrace it, allowing their teammate to release it before moving from a fast jog to an all-out sprint. Until that release, they hold back, focusing primarily on the baton and secondarily on the finish line.

This baton represents success. For some of us, we try to carry a baton someone has passed off but not fully released to us. We remain focused on guarding that person's idea of success more than on pursuing God's destination for us. We remain tied to their pacing, their process, and their procedures. I continued to hold on to a baton of big things and perfection. That baton felt excruciatingly heavy, and trying to run with it wore me out.

My parents' definition of success felt to me like an unreachable finish line. Maybe your church culture defines a godly woman in a certain way. Perhaps you have allowed a boss, mentor, or business guru to cloud God's definition of success in your life. Yes, God placed within you—gifts with which he longs for you to run freely and sense his pleasure as you strain forward. But some of us haven't firmly grasped the baton, released the previous runner, and settled into our rhythms. We keep dragging others' expectations along behind us.

Pause and Reflect

Are you carrying somebody else's baton of success, and is it slowing you down? Write down the primary influences in your life. In a sentence or two, define what success means to you. Prayerfully ask God where these ideas first took root in your heart and mind.

There's a deeper reason we must define what success is in our lives. Until you release your baton over to Christ, it's hard to get an accurate view of success. Christ must become the power behind your pacing, process, and procedures.

With Christ-defining success, we can say, "This is the finish line You're pointing me towards, Lord, and I'm willing to run with everything I've got."

A Successful Finish

When I ran cross country in high school, our coach used to take us down to the beach for training, and we ran from pier to pier. Running in the sand proved grueling, but one thing pushed us forward—you could always visualize the finish line. The vast pier jutting into the sea remained constantly in view. The goal was closer with each breath, pump of arms, and pound of the foot. I often sensed God whispering in the wind, "Keep going. Don't give up. I'm right here with you."

However, I often could not visualize the finish line in our three-mile cross-country races. We ran through parks, neighborhoods, and trails. As providence would have it, our last meet of the season took place at a park along the ocean. I needed a specific score to advance to the finals, and I grinned when the coach announced the location. Race day came, and my time stayed steady. I ran at a pace to meet my time goal easily. And then I saw it. The race's last leg included a steep cliff with the finish line at the bluff. The wind stilled, and I felt like I could not suck in enough air. My emotions vacillated between fear, defeat, and determination. I had not planned on this cliff. I wondered if I had the energy for it.

That's the trouble with leadership. We don't always know what's around the next bend. And once we see it, we become flooded with doubt, yet we still need to encourage those following us to keep running with us. My entire team followed me up that cliff. If I quit, others might too. I've learned to love running up the cliffs. That terrain forces me to face the reality of my inability. It will take the work of God to get me to the top.

Relaxing Your Lack in His More Than Enough

We rest in God's ability, because we serve a God who always finishes what he starts. I've always loved the prophecy in the book of Zechariah concerning Zerubbabel and

Solomon's temple destroyed by the Babylonians. As the Israelites stood looking at the looming task of rebuilding, the job seemed insurmountable. This temple was one of the world's ancient wonders. It had stood in perfection on the mount in Jerusalem.

Zerubbabel and those he led did not have the tools or skill to replicate its beauty and constructing something of lesser grandeur felt fruitless. They held onto Solomon's definition of success instead of embracing God's design for a new temple. They felt too many obstacles stood before them and lacked the energy to finish the job. God spoke to both objections of inadequacy—lack of both skills and tools—and the people did indeed finish the temple.

It may not have appeared as magnificent as Solomon's, but the Lord would bless it.

"You can't force these things. They only come about through my Spirit" (Zechariah 4:6 The Message).

I've learned to embrace God's response to my objections. When I don't feel my work is magnificent enough to be labeled as successful, I cry, "God bless it!" And when I lack the energy, ability, or impetus to keep running my race or completing the task, I cling to, "His Spirit will enable me to finish."

I entered that last leg of the race set to place in the top fifteen. Not first place, but good enough for me to proceed to finals. God was with me—he would get me there, gale storm or gust. He would get the glory. Ultimately, don't we all want our success to be a God story? We rest in knowing our placement or achievement, wherever it might be, is God's plan.

Look at God's promise regarding the temple should Zerubbabel remain faithful to finish: "The latter glory of this house shall be greater than the former, says the Lord of hosts. And in this place I will give peace, declares the Lord of hosts" (Haggai 2:9 ESV).

When we choose to be faithful to the finish, God will bestow his glory and bring peace.

Pause and Reflect

In what ways does your success align with God's divine plan? Do you ever feel your work is not magnificent or spectacular enough? What are some ways that this perception has stifled you?

I recall the day I was invited to Moody Publishers to meet the team. As I buttoned up my coat to catch my cab, my hands began to shake, I felt my stomach muscles tighten, and sweat break out across my forehead. I looked at my friend Kim. "I can't go there. They will take one look at me and feel like they made a mistake publishing me. Tell them I got sick!" She looked at me and said, "That is nothing but a lie from the pit of hell. You are going, and they will love you as much as I do. Now, march, lady!" (Don't we all need a Kim in our lives?)

When I arrived at Moody, I walked beside the bookshelves with countless books written by many of my spiritual heroes—Spurgeon, Moody, Tozer, Pink. And there on the same shelves sat a book with my name on the cover. Inconceivable. I fought back the tears. I was experiencing a capstone moment in my life, and I allowed worry and fear to consume me.

That night after returning to our hotel, when I laid my head down on the pillow, I sensed God whisper, "It's time to let me bring healing from self-doubt into your life." The tears poured down my cheeks, and I muttered, "God, I hand this all over to you and ask you to do whatever you need. That's when God began to build my life upon a new foundation of grace. God would bless my effort, even when it seemed to lack the glory of Solomon's temple. He would enable me to finish whatever good work he had for me, even when I felt like I lacked the skill or the necessary resources. By the power of his Holy Spirit, I will finish every race.

I love this quote from Winston Churchill. "Success is not final. Failure is not fatal. It's the courage to continue that counts." But I love this senior quote from my daughter when she graduated high school even more. "There is no failure. You either succeed or you learn."

Today's success may seem minor or less grandiose than you imagined. You may feel unable to keep running—out of breath, ill-equipped, and lacking resources. Take courage. God will get you to the finish line and the glory will be beyond what you ever envisioned.

Pause and Reflect

What personal shortcomings do you most often bring up to God? How does God's promise to Zerubbabel—that his Spirit would accomplish the work necessary—encourage you?

Crossing the Finish Line

In most areas of influence, we equate knowledge with leadership. We follow experts, guides, and gurus. But as a leader, I've discovered the most intelligent person in the room is not the person who knows the most. It's the person who knows what they don't know. They humbly admit their weakness and are intelligent enough to collaborate with someone from whom they can learn and grow. That is the true leader—one who seeks out people from whom she can learn. Zerubbabel co-labored with Ezra and Nehemiah to finish the temple.

Maybe you are unsure of what it takes to reach your finish line. You don't have to know every step. Learn to surround yourself with those who can help you finish well. Every runner has a coach. Some have exercise therapists, nutritionists, running partners, sports psychologists, etc. No top-level runner trains without help. And no leader leads without help, either. Remember this promise from Christ,

> **"My grace is sufficient for you, for my power is made perfect in weakness" (2 Corinthians 12:9 NIV).**

I love the movie *Chariots of Fire.* It's about a young man named Eric Liddell, an incredibly gifted runner, and a devout follower of Jesus. His sister felt he would serve better on the mission field instead of becoming a track star. (Notice the different definitions of success?) My favorite line in the movie is: When I run, I sense his pleasure. Liddell refused to cave to his sister's definition of success. He knew what God had created him to do and remained committed to it.

Run your race. Heaven is smiling.

Leading in Prayer

Heavenly Father, I'm tired of striving to reach an elusive bar of success that I know was not set by you. Show me the unique giftings you wish to activate within me for your glory. Help me disconnect from the voice in my head that says I need to do more and be more—you are already proud of me. I have nothing to prove. I will diligently run the race you've uniquely designed for me—this is the true definition of success. Amen.

"There is no failure.
You either succeed
or you learn."

-Eliana Wiggenhorn

Asbury University Student

A Letter to the Sisters Declaring "I'm a Nobody"

Precious Sister

Sometimes we confuse what feels true with what is true.

For example, what if I told you that your worth was priceless? That you are a rare masterpiece, valuable beyond comprehension? And what if I told you that you were distinctively gifted and assigned for a grand purpose? You may accept those statements as true or some inner insecurity may rise, nervously bristle, and reject the notion. It will challenge the thought that your contribution to the world is unique, priceless, and great. If it doesn't feel true or even look true, you may disregard that God created you as a part of his most valuable crowning achievement.

But I'm nobody special," you counter. I'm just a mom, a school aide, a salesclerk, an office manager. Compared to other women who are on the front lines of leading and experiencing amazing success, it's tempting to minimize your significance. I don't have much to offer. Others are better than me, so let them do it.

First, don't compare yourself to anyone else. You're a one-of-a-kind creation. The only comparison you should ever make is with yourself. Make sure you're better this year than you were last year. Be the best version of yourself possible. Second, don't diminish your place in this world. You have influence and you have a voice. You are a leader. Someone is always watching. You have opportunities everywhere to shine and impact your home, community, city, state, and this planet. As Marianne Williamson wrote, "Your playing small does not serve the world." (quote is taken from Marianne Williamson's poem "Our Deepest Fear," in her book ***A Return to Love.***)

It's true.

You're wonderfully and remarkably made. Once you get that truth down on the inside of you and accept it as fact, your mindset will transform. Fears and insecurities move aside as your inner genius is unleashed to step up. Your new outlook will inform your actions and behaviors.

Instead of "I can't and I'm not," you'll be declaring, "I can, and I will."

Dawn Damon is a high-performance Mentor & Transformational Coach at BraveHeartMentor.

dawndamon.com

www.bravehearted woman.com

CHAPTER 5

Value The Gift You Hold

Kymberli Joye

Kymberli Joye is a vocal artist and worship leader who skyrocketed to public recognition as a contestant on *The Voice*. Since her time on the show, Kymberli has been in music and ministry full-time, traveling the country as a guest worship leader.

Kymberli recently began to worship collectively with songwriters from the New England area called The Huddle Worship. They released their first album last year, "Coming Off the Bench."

I remember a moment as a contestant on *The Voice* when they asked us who we would like to sing with if we made it to the finale. Without hesitation, the first person on my list was gospel music powerhouse, CeCe Winans. CeCe is one of my biggest vocal influences. I look up to her, not just because of her fantastic voice, but for her kindness and humility. Fast forward to 2021, my friend Freddy Washington asked me to sing a few songs in a three-night production called Christmas on Broadway at Times Square Church in New York. You can imagine my excitement upon realizing that CeCe was the special guest. As we ended the final song, CeCe turned around, pointed to me, and said, "Hey, come out and sing this with me." I don't know how I got there, but I somehow managed to walk toward her. I was nervous at first, but it all came so naturally. It was an incredible moment. After the concert, she took extra time to sit and talk with us. And you know, God is so good because even though I didn't make it to *The Voice* finale to sing with my favorite vocalist, he gave me that full-circle moment. It was his perfectly orchestrated timing.

Authentically Me

I grew up singing in the church where my parents were pastors. My mother was the worship leader, and I was truthfully more content to sing in the background. I remember the day she said, "Kymberli, I want you to lead this song." While I was confident in my ability to sing the song, I was also incredibly nervous. I realized leading people in worship was much different from singing a song alone.

The first time I led worship, I was all over the place. Nobody connected, but I did my best. The congregation was so gracious. Each Sunday, I was more nervous than the week before. That didn't stop my mother, though. I finally asked her, "Why do you continue to push me to do this?"

She replied, "Because it's time for you to lead." When I told her I didn't know how, she said, "You can't lead as I lead. You have to lead as you lead." I've taken those words with me and used them in every leadership position I've had.

Today, I have the privilege of leading worship for several churches from Connecticut to Boston, and even North Carolina. I've learned each church has a different worship style and culture. So, I try to study that as much as possible while leading from who I am. I must share authentically and honor the gift I've been given.

It reminds me of the story in the Bible of David when he brings his brothers' lunch to the front lines while they're waging a battle and waiting in fear because of a big giant named Goliath. Suddenly David says, "Why isn't anybody fighting him?" Because everybody was afraid, they did nothing.

King Saul sees this and tells David, " If you fight and kill the giant, you will be the most famous man in the kingdom. I'll reward you and let you marry my daughter." So courageous David is all in. Saul gives him his armor to fight the giant, but it's too big. Since David is small, he decides to take off the armor and use what he has—a simple slingshot, a stone, and his faith. If David defeated a giant, I can shoot for the same courage and confidence in my life.

All I have is what God has given me, nothing more and nothing less; this is the precious place I lead from no matter the position in which I'm serving. It could mean leading worship in a small intimate group or an arena with 5,000 people. I don't have to worry as long as I go in the grace and faith God has given me.

If we hone in on the gifts God has given us, we begin to understand why we are in these positions. God has ordered our steps, and we are precisely placed. Embrace it. God has given you a unique voice, perspective, and vision for what's to come. As long as you're following God, you will be fine.

Pause and Reflect

Envision yourself in the competition of a lifetime. If you could work with someone at the top of your industry, who would it be and why? In what three ways are you uniquely you, in comparison?

Hand it Over

To lead well, I've had to delegate my responsibilities. I continue to lead as worship pastor for my parents' church. They have allowed me to travel and use my gift all over the country. I ensure there's a team in place, so things run smoothly in my absence. I also have an incredible team that handles my bookings and travel arrangements. It's less stressful to know I only need to focus on being in the moment and leading.

When I lead worship, I pray first to make sure it is something God has assigned me to do and not just what I want to do. Even if it is a yes, I want to know if there is an overall goal. I often ask God, "What do you want me to bring to this assignment?" Sometimes my plate can get plenty full, but I know if God has given me the green light, he will also give me the capacity to handle it.

Pause and Reflect

Do you find yourself overwhelmed with the pressure of trying to do it yourself? Do you have a team strong in their own giftedness? Are there specific tasks that could be given to someone else, making your load lighter so you can focus on ministry?

Legacy and Limits

The blessings I've experienced do not come from my own efforts, but from the prayers of people before me. My grandparents prayed continuously that their legacy would continue through their children and grandchildren. They prayed their family would love God with all their hearts and bring honor to him through ministry. I know it brings my parents joy to see their children successfully living their dreams for God. Because of their prayers, I know God continues to use, build, and equip me. Therefore, I can walk in this lane with faith.

Leadership means knowing when to say no. No is a complete sentence. As Christians, if we say no, it can leave us feeling bad because we don't want to be mean or insensitive to the need. When our hearts are in the right place, we realize sometimes saying no is because God hasn't called us to it. God knows when there are too many items on our to-do lists. There's a reason the Bible says on the seventh day, he rested. We need to take time to rest and recuperate. If we don't, we'll burn ourselves out and be no good to anyone. It's okay to say no, and it's okay to stand in confidence with your decision.

Pause and Reflect

In what ways can you honor the legacy and prayers of those who came before you? If you haven't established criteria for determining what you can or cannot take on, make time now to devise a plan.

You Are His Plan

As a woman, it's common to struggle while standing in the place of leadership because of societal views and norms. Yet, throughout the Word of God, he used women to advance his message. I repeat the story often of when Jesus rose from the dead. The first people to get the news were women. It's not unnatural for you to be a leader—it's truly a gift he's given you. You can lead in every area of your life including church, community, and even home. Your leadership might even look like supporting someone, another ministry, your spouse, or your pastor. That's leading from humility.

Pause and Reflect

Have you met resistance as a woman in leadership due to societal views and norms? How can you embrace the biblical legacy of female leaders? List different ways you are positioned to lead in all aspects of your life?

Leading in Prayer

Heavenly Father, I am grateful for the legacy and prayer of those who have gone before me. Help me identify where I am fit to lead, giving me the courage to walk into those places confidently. Create in me the ability to recognize your perfect timing and the wisdom to discern when to say no. May all that I do be for your glory. Amen.

"When I stand before God at the end of my life, I would hope that I would not have a single bit of talent left, and could say, 'I used everything you gave me.'"

–Erma Bombeck

Humorist, Newspaper Columnist & News Correspondent

CHAPTER 6

Know Timing is Everything

Gigi Orsillo

Actress Gigi Orsillo studied Communications, TV, and Film at Oral Roberts University in her hometown of Tulsa, Oklahoma. Shortly after, Gigi moved to California and continued training at the prestigious Groundlings Studio and Playhouse West for stage and screen. Gigi has served as a host for the Starz network, TBN, and IGN and has appeared nationwide in commercial and print ads.

Since appearing in the spy comedy *Sleeper Agent*, Gigi has quickly made her mark in faith-based films. She has appeared in TV projects and feature films, including *Running the Bases, Family Camp,* and the Pureflix 2023 series *Fragment: Oblivion.* Gigi's three daughters, Eliana, Preslie, and London, have also caught the acting bug. Her passion is pointing people to Jesus and pursuing faith-based projects and opportunities that impact the visual arts.

You could say I was born into the spotlight. Cast in my first commercial when I was two and a half, simply because I was in the right place at the right time. It was a Christmas commercial for a local mall in Tulsa that continued to air for 20 years. I grew up on set and always loved a good production. My dad was a director and a producer. My mom was a makeup artist and wardrobe stylist. The movie world felt like home to me, so I pursued television and film as an adult. My biggest influence is my mom. She loves Jesus and has a very firm faith. She was there in my doubts and struggles, praying for me and giving me wisdom and counsel. I am blessed to have had her support every single day. Even with that support, it was essential to learn that my faith must be my faith. I couldn't solely depend on her walk with the Lord. Seeing the example she modeled helped me lean wholly on God.

I've always wanted to glorify God with my talents. While I don't want to do anything that would compromise my faith, I have enjoyed working on secular projects. In those productions, I've worked side-by-side with the crew and cast members who don't share my faith in Christ. God allows me to be light in the darkness. There have been working environments that felt really dark, yet I knew I was working where God wanted me to be. I have been a part of conversations allowing me to talk about God's faithfulness and character. In those moments, I realized I was present at the right time.

Working with a faith-based production team is fulfilling in a totally different way. Not everyone on set knows Jesus, and that, too, presents an opportunity to be light. Faith-based productions create a unique working atmosphere because you align yourself with people who pray. I lean upon my faith in Christ in this industry full of no's and disappointments. I can get really excited about an upcoming role. Still, it's always disappointing when an audition doesn't result in being cast. It builds my faith to remember that I'm called and equipped by God. The confirmation of my calling affirms me no matter the outcome. I may have started acting because it was the family business, but the reason I continued after moving to LA was that I had the desire to make a difference and walk in the gifts God gave me.

Pause and Reflect

Were you impacted by someone or something in your childhood that influenced and shaped your calling today? How do you actively demonstrate your trust in God during times of rejection? List three ways to walk in faith and lean on God's promises for your life.

The Role of a Lifetime

Once I started having children, I felt God say, "Go ahead and trust me with your career." By faith, I stopped acting when my daughters were young. I've watched them grow into young women with their own faith and spiritual foundation, which is beautiful.

Motherhood introduced me to some of the most significant role models. There are six of us within a group of homeschooling mothers. But nobody's ever just a mom. I think it's such an amazing calling to be a mother. When I struggle as a parent, my conversations with these women lead me to the cross. They have had a profound influence on my life.

Ten years into my motherhood journey, I reached out to a friend I had worked with on a TV show. He was directing his first feature film, and I wanted to tell him how proud I was of his achievement. When he encouraged me to audition, my response was a firm, "No." I explained I was a mom now and didn't really act anymore. He reminded me that God had given me a gift, and he hadn't taken it away because I had become a mother. I thought about it and realized he was right. I auditioned and ended up doing that little film. On the set, I felt real peace. I was where I was supposed to be, recognizing that God gave me the ability to do the job. He's continued to help me connect with the characters I play and bring them to life.

Today's faith-based films have grown in quality and influence. It's been amazing God-timing for me to reenter the industry. I feel blessed to be where I'm supposed to be at the time God wanted it to happen.

Pause and Reflect

Reflect on and list the ways you have trusted God in the midst of taking a break from your passions or goals due to a change in direction, responsibilities, or unforeseen circumstances?

What Matters Most

It's easy to think we must do something big and great to be influential. Truthfully, our most significant influence is our daily interactions—our kids, friends, and anyone we meet. Sharing a smile at the grocery store can influence someone to have a better day. Bringing joy and showing sincere interest in people can impact many lives.

God made us to show others they are loved by him—being his hands and feet. And it's an enormous responsibility. Even if you're not on a stage, your story can touch people that my story cannot. It's amazing that God chooses to use our stories to change people's lives. Fear and shame can sometimes hold me back from sharing my struggles. God uses my transparency when I push through that fear by being honest and open about my situation. People can connect with our story, and we can lead them to the true source of healing and restoration. Sharing Jesus and filling up heaven is the greatest responsibility on this earth and thinking about being a part of this—gives me so much joy.

When you truly trust in God and desire to use everything he's given you to honor him, you will not miss what he has for you. "In all your ways acknowledge Him, and He will make your paths straight" (Proverbs 3:6 NASB). Know that he's got a plan, and he's got you—he just needs your willing heart.

Leading in Prayer

Heavenly Father, I thank you for my journey and story. When I experience rejection and disappointment, remind me of who I am in you. Direct my steps, helping me to know that in every season, even when aspects of life are paused, your plans are with purpose. Continue to help me transparently share and introduce others to you. Amen.

"God's answers to opportunities we are presented with will be YES, NO or WAIT. You have to be willing to hear His answer and be content with His response."

-Natasha Owens

Recording Artist

CHAPTER 7

Live in Courageous Vulnerability

Janell Rardon

Pain can be a powerful tool if it inspires positive transformational change in our lives. Janell Rardon, MA, is a Board-Certified Life Coach (AACC) encouraging those who have experienced trauma to live and lead authentically.

Whether sharing her weekly *Heartlift* podcast, life coaching, or writing, Janell utilizes her journey through trauma to lead others into healing. Her award-winning book, *Stronger Every Day: 9 Tools for an Emotionally Healthy You* (Revell Books), equips readers with intentional emotional health tools to build better relationships.

When I was young, I didn't understand I was traumatized. My mother was a dancer in her day and volunteered at the USO when she was in the Marines. When we were stationed in Norfolk, Virginia, my repertoire expanded to dance and acrobatics, all while twirling that shiny, silver baton. Instead of finding secure attachment at home, it seems I found it performing. With an absent, alcoholic father, I found the applause, approval, and affirmation on the stage to be the source of my self-worth and identity.

I didn't see that all this effort I was putting in to earn my father's and mother's approval, as well as my internal need to fix them, was not normal. I didn't realize my childhood experiences were crippling me emotionally. I would have to fight my way to the truth. In vulnerable honesty, I'd yet to discover how to live freely in the liberty of Christ and his calling on my life.

When I started my training in counseling, I discovered a profound truth about trauma. Simply put, trauma is when a person's emotions are too big for their own body. It doesn't matter if the "t" in trauma is a big "T" or a little "t." Trauma is trauma. I often meet people who minimize their story, saying, "It could have been so much worse." I understand because I used to minimize my trauma, too. Living in a highly dysfunctional home deeply imprinted on my little psyche. When you are not seen, heard, or known, when you don't feel like you belong or are not safe and secure, the whole trajectory of your life is different. I came into life with an emotional disability, which we would explain in the world of therapeutic counseling as disordered attachments. When you do not have a secure attachment, you feel you're not good enough. You look outside of yourself for acceptance. I searched for something that would make me feel good about myself.

As we grow in Christ, we develop secure attachments. Unfortunately, many of us continue to limp like Jacob after he completed a wrestling match with an angel (Genesis 32). Growing older, I recognized the effects of my trauma more clearly. I became super high functioning on the outside to prove my value, worth, and dignity. I thought, By golly, if I do this, my daddy will stop drinking. If I win this, mommy will be happy. It is the subconscious work of every child to want to please and make their parents proud, no matter what kind of parents they are.

For so long, I didn't know what to do with the pain. I didn't know I was broken. I mean, I knew it. But I didn't know what to do with it because I was not given the information, education, or tools. Alcoholics Anonymous and Alanon were available, but presumably, if not for my mother's pride, shame, and perhaps the weight of working and providing for the family, I could have learned skills to help change my life.

Later in life, I traveled and ministered in Thailand, where I learned a cultural saying, "Keep the fire inside the house." It helped me understand that perhaps that is how my mother felt. But if we don't let the fire out of the house and choose to hide the flames with a facade of perfection, our house will burn down.

Pause and Reflect

Are you aware of any unhealed trauma in your life? Do you live in a ***house on fire***, covering up trauma to protect the image of your home life? In what ways are you trying to earn your worth? In what ways do you minimize your trauma?

Keeping the Past out of the Present

As I grew into adulthood and became a parent, I did not want to bring my past into my children's futures.

Vigilance is key. Nothing changes until you increase your awareness and reach your threshold. Once you realize you don't want your children to relive your experiences, and you don't want a dysfunctional home, circumstances will change. When your awareness becomes a prayer, God births a miracle. He begins the transformation.

As leaders, we often tell ourselves we must eliminate the negative patterns of trauma before being qualified to help others. However, personal healing is a continual process rooted in vulnerability, vigilance, and prayer.

Many years into my journey, I still grapple with the idea of success, even in the professional counseling industry. I must really muster the courage to truly be who I am and say what I need to say—and not just say what everyone would expect me to say. I think I'll be in that battle for the rest of my life.

Pause and Reflect

List how past traumas have affected you and your family negatively and positively. How can you be more purposeful in using your trauma to strengthen your relationships?

Vulnerably Secure

"Don't be vulnerable because you'll get wounded if you're vulnerable" was often reinforced in my young life. I didn't understand that. It is in the wounding that great leaders are created. Yes, the shame is there. Often, leaders have to learn to walk beyond the shame of their past to find freedom from the pain and guilt of the past. Formation of our character takes place in the hard spaces of the crucible—the pit, the lions' den, the belly of the whale experiences of life. We learn that being vulnerable with our story becomes our strength.

In leading, we can dive back into our own story to help someone with their journey. However, as a leader with a public platform, it is imperative to use extreme wisdom and discretion when sharing your personal story. Using discretion shows integrity and honor for the people (family, friends, or distant acquaintances) involved in your testimony, even when you feel they don't deserve it. Learning to align with the Father puts us in a position to gain discretionary wisdom from him. It's between you and God how much of your story you tell. What people think about your story is between them and God. It is not meant for you to carry. Knowing Christ and who he says we are helps us to live in fearless security.

If I live to my fullest capacity today in overcoming insecurities, I'll have more potential tomorrow. When we know better, we can do better. In our awareness, we can shine more brilliantly. Leading with vulnerable security in who we are, helps us to walk into a room or show up in a Zoom meeting and change the atmosphere. Imagine what we can do as influencers on all levels if we are secure in who we are—who God says we are in him.

Pause and Reflect

What is standing in the way of telling your story? Is there a part of your story that brings you shame? How can vulnerability strengthen your testimony? What boundaries can you set in your life to use discretion and honor those involved in your story?

Three Transformative Questions

Do you feel called to leadership but are afraid your family legacy is standing in your way? I want you to ask yourself three questions to help change dysfunctional generational patterns.

1. Do I know God?

If we've formed our ideas about God through the voices of spiritual leaders only, we miss out on a personal revelation of the Father. Knowing him for ourselves is the ultimate goal. This knowledge comes from building deep faith, which frames our understanding of God's character.

2. Do I know myself?

So many voices compete for our attention, and sometimes they become louder than our own. You must know the sound of your voice to understand your inherent worth. One of the most significant hurdles in my life is allowing the voices of everyone in the world, but mine, to lead my life. As I've learned to know my true voice—the voice that God gave me—I've equated it with value, self-worth, and dignity.

3. How do I define success?

The world's definition of success differs greatly from the Father's. Finding where your understanding of success aligns with God's nature is critical. Deuteronomy 10:12 gives excellent insight into God-defined success.

"...what do you think God expects from you? Just this: Live in his presence in holy reverence, follow the road he sets out for you, love him, serve God, your God, with everything you have in you" (The Message).

Pause and Reflect

Did you have trouble answering any of the above-listed transformative questions? State why by writing out your answers. What steps can you take to redefine your understanding of who God is, who you are, and his definition of success?

Leading in Prayer

Heavenly Father, I ask you to be with me today. Vulnerability can be scary. Help me be vigilant against negative thoughts and embrace my story without fear. I will not sweep pain under the rug or minimize it to find acceptance in the eyes of others. Thank you for refining the leader you've designed me to be—who boasts about my weakness for your glory. Amen.

"Vulnerability is the birthplace of innovation, creativity and change."

-Dr. Brené Brown

Professor, Lecturer, & Podcast Host

A Letter to the Sisters who Feel "My Broken Past Disqualifies Me From Ministry"

Precious Sister

I see you. Sitting in the back row, one step away from the exit. You long for an invitation to the ministry table. Only there's the voice that whispers, Who do you think you are? God can't use the damaged, the sinful, or the broken.

I have some good news. Your invitation to ministry has arrived. Because the last time I checked, God specializes in using exactly these kinds of people to build his kingdom.

Damaged: Consider the Samaritan woman, shacked up with man number five and hiding in plain sight at a well at high noon. But when she encountered Jesus' love, shame fell away, and she fulfilled her calling as an evangelist to the people who rejected her. Instead of concealing your deepest shame, you can offer it as God's tool to free others powerfully.

Sinful: There was the woman who had lived a sinful life from Luke 7:36-50. She entered the house of Simon the Pharisee because she heard Jesus was there, then lavishly poured out costly perfume and tears for the love of Jesus. Pointing to her selfless worship, Jesus taught a prideful Pharisee about the power of grace.

Broken: Remember Peter, the disciple who denied Jesus three times? When Jesus forgave Peter's betrayal and healed his broken heart, he released a powerhouse of grace and love that catapulted Peter into his calling as a fearless apostle. Your greatest failure, redeemed by Jesus' forgiveness, can become the rocket fuel that propels you toward restoring other broken people.

Your Past Is Your Platform: A few years ago, I watched these truths unfold in the life of a woman I'll call Catherine. At 17, she became pregnant and chose abortion. Catherine never got over the shame of having ended the life of her child, and the enemy used this secret sin to tell her, "Your brokenness disqualifies you from ever being used by God." But when Catherine received God's forgiveness and finally forgave herself, he brought so many post-abortive women to her that she launched a ministry addressing their unique needs.

Sister, it's time to banish the lying voice keeping you in the back row–wearing the labels Disqualified, Excluded, and Not Good Enough.

If you listen carefully, you will hear God's voice saying, "Arise, my beloved daughter. Now confessed and redeemed, your past becomes your platform to pursue other damaged daughters, sinful sisters, and broken beloveds. They are waiting for hope. Find them and lead them out of darkness into my marvelous light with the truth of who I was for you in the dark. And surely, I am with you to the end of the age."

Lynne Rienstra (lynnerienstra.com) has served Samaritan's Purse as a Regional Director for Church Engagement since 2013. Impacting pastors and church leaders in 14 states, Lynne has witnessed Samaritan's Purse on the ground worldwide.

Lynne and husband Rob serve Trinity Presbyterian Church (PCA) in Covington, Georgia. They have two married children and three granddaughters.

CHAPTER 8

Let the Golden Rule Guide You

Monica Schmelter

The Golden Rule principle, "Do unto others as you would have them do unto you," is woven throughout Monica Schmelter's life. Monica, best known as the well-loved host of the Christian Television Network's daily program, Bridges, has been on the air for over 25 years. Broadcast weekly in over 50 million homes across the U.S. This inspiring talk show highlights Christian struggles and triumphs in living everyday life. It is a project that represents Monica's childhood dream of using television to make a difference in the world. While she enjoys working in media, speaking, and writing books, her happiest place is spending time with family.

When I started in leadership, I thought my traits as a kind and loving person would not fare so well. Traditionally, the expectations for men and women in leadership vary greatly. Society typically respects men in an assertive or even aggressive role. As the first female General Manager at Christian Television Network, I was struggling with the thought of being ruthless or leading more aggressively to gain respect. Thinking I was always right and setting unrealistic expectations made it difficult to have a good relationship with people. I always believed in the golden rule but did not apply this to ministry or business.

The transmitter frequently went out during the early years of the old WHTN building. My team worked hard, and I sensed their discouragement. The verse from Matthew 7:12 came to life for me—to treat others how I want to be treated. A heightened sense of compassion and kindness bubbled up through affirmation and encouragement. I now understood God designed us to work as a body—as a team. The more honor and kindness I gave to every person, the more encouraged and motivated they were. This helped us get the gospel out in more ways than before.

I long for God to work through the real me. Jesus modeled servant leadership and kindness. He was meek and his strength was under the restraint of the Holy Spirit. When I leaned into that, I began to celebrate kindness through my authentic self. **I lead kind. I lead well.** God continues refining my leadership style, and I am thankful for his work through me.

Pause and Reflect

Treating others like we want to be treated requires intentionality. Where does your life need to shine the Golden

Rule? List benefits of adopting a servant leadership style. What characteristics or practices would you change as you implement servant leadership into your daily God-mission? Write down how God challenges you to grow in this area?

Clear Communication is Kindness

I used to live with rage, causing me to lash out and speak harshly to people. With the help of the Holy Spirit, I now practice kind and clear communication. This essential practice includes setting well-defined expectations and ensuring my team understands the desired outcome.

If we are honest, we all have lost our cool. The Bible says when we are tempted, He will show us the way of escape (1 Corinthians 10:13). Removing myself from the situation gives me the space to tend to my mental health before returning to the matter at hand.

As a leader, I may upset people with my decisions or how I lead. Insecurity makes that difficult. When others are not so kind to me or communicate by gossiping, I choose to acknowledge uncomfortable feelings. I also realize amid my brokenness; I am whole in Christ. He will help keep those feelings from causing us emotional damage. Rather than sweeping issues under the rug, it helps to remain intentional when facing difficulties and conflict.

Pause and Reflect

Can you recognize a time when you lost your cool? What difference would it make in your life if you paused to seek the help of the Holy Spirit? What are the ways God can help you tend to your health and work environment during those heated moments?

Kindness is Not Playing Favorites

A balanced leader remains unbiased in team relationships. Leaders must remain aware of the consequences. Ultimately, in playing favorites, someone is reduced to being an outsider. Even though I love and respect my team, becoming too close to a coworker makes friendships and work performance evaluations difficult.

Kind leadership sets a precedent with open communication, outlined expectations, written performance plans, and opportunities for improvement. Titus 2:11-12 gives us a biblical comparison between self-control and the desire to control others.

"For the grace of God has appeared that offers salvation to all people. It teaches us to say 'No' to ungodliness and worldly passions, and to live self-controlled, upright and godly lives in this present age ..." (NIV).

Setting boundaries early in our role as leaders creates a precedent for having healthy conversations if goals are unmet. Regrettably, should a team member not meet these expectations, I must prepare my heart for a professional parting of ways. It's difficult and takes its toll on a leader's heart. I walk through these moments prayerfully.

Pause and Reflect

In professionally approaching your work relationships, do you have checks and balances in place? Has favoritism negatively affected a working relationship? Boundaries left unchecked propel our natural desires to run roughshod over others. Is God speaking to you about a specific area where you have crossed the line with your professional versus social life?

Kindness Begins with a Humble Heart

There is no place for a diva mentality in leadership. When pride says people will not respect my leadership if I own a mistake, I remember the only perfect leader was Jesus.

Recently, a former employee returned to WHTN. Upon reconnecting, I discovered he felt cast aside and not given the opportunities offered to other employees. Even though I could not recall the specifics, I apologized. I would never intentionally hurt anyone. I made a poor decision and owned up to my mistake. When somebody else messes up, I would much rather they bring it to my attention with an apology. When we address these issues with kindness, the Holy Spirit leads us to repentance and reconciliation.

"And all of this is a gift from God, who brought us back to himself through Christ. And God has given us this task of reconciling people to him. For God was in Christ, reconciling the world to himself, no longer counting people's sins against them. And he gave us this wonderful message of reconciliation" (2 Corinthians 5:18-19 NLT).

A kind leader is never self-absorbed, unapproachable, or difficult to please.

Serving alongside everyone, regardless of the task, helps maintain a humble heart. I pray regularly for the team, asking God to show me their giftings and talents and for the wisdom to develop them. One of our team members has a video podcast with a brand-new beautiful set. I feel privileged and overwhelmed with joy to be a part of leading and launching a new ministry. I am happy this team member is at the forefront. Matching the gifts and talents of my team with who I am is key. This approach kicks diva-hood to the curb.

Pause and Reflect

Have you ever allowed pride to hurt a professional relationship? What steps can/did you take to bring reconciliation, demonstrating a humble heart? Are you easily approachable? How do you respond when it's brought to your attention that you've made a mistake?

How can you extend grace when a team member makes a mistake?

Keeping it Together

Twenty-six years ago, I made a professional commitment to myself. I decided it wouldn't be beneficial to shed tears in the middle of a work-related conflict. When I come close, I stick with a concise response. It is unnecessary to be disrespectful and raise my voice. Everyone at WHTN understands. My team also knows I will kindly end our working relationship if they disrespect what we are doing.

In my early years, I thought it was the Christian thing to be accessible to all our viewers. During an encouraging conversation on social media, a viewer scolded me for not giving her my cell number. Rather than raising my voice, I kindly diffused the situation. She appreciated my offer for an occasional chat online. Proverbs 15:1 reinforces that we shouldn't allow someone's anger or negative thoughts to cause us to sin.

> **"A soft answer turns away wrath, but a harsh word stirs up anger" (ESV).**

Pause and Reflect

How do you keep it together in the face of heightened emotions? Have you ever regretted using harsh words in the workplace? What could you have done to diffuse the conflict instead?

Respecting Your Limits and the Limits of Others is Kindness

I titled a chapter in one of my books, 'No Is a Complete Answer.' When someone asks me if I can do something and I must say, 'No,' I do not always give them an explanation.

With kindness, I express my appreciation and simply tell them I cannot do whatever they ask. Respecting our limits protects us.

My work involves a tremendous number of moving pieces. Some days, it seems everyone wants something from me. It is not possible to meet every need. I do it if someone higher up asks me to do something reasonable. I may need to explain my workload and work with them on re-prioritizing my projects. I do not just take all that on without being honest.

When I assign a project to my team, I ask them to tell me honestly how long they expect the project to take. I will also ask them if they can work within the project timetable. I set the standards and expectations for my team.

In Matthew 5:33-37, Jesus says, "And don't say anything you don't mean. This counsel is embedded deep in our traditions. You only make things worse when you lay down a smoke screen of pious talk, saying, 'I'll pray for you,' and never doing it, or saying, 'God be with you,' and not meaning it. You don't make your words true by embellishing them with religious lace. In making your speech sound more religious, it becomes less true. Just say 'yes' and 'no.' When you manipulate words to get your own way, you go wrong" (The Message).

Pause and Reflect

Make a list of people to whom you have difficulty saying ***No***. How can you respect your limits, as well as the limitations of others, with kindness?

Kindly Take an Attitude Check

Hebrews 4:16 says we can come boldly to God for mercy and grace in our time of need. When I lack kindness, it indicates that I have crossed a line. It shows that I'm leading in my strength rather than leaning upon God. In these moments, I realize I cannot manage one more item.

I might need to take a mental health day or an extra hour before starting work. Either way, I have learned I must take care of myself. When I see that red flag, I realize I have not loved my neighbors because I have not loved myself. We are at the end of ourselves and out of Holy Spirit power. This does not mean we are terrible people or horrible leaders. We recognize we need to fill up our gas tank. There is a problem here. I have been leaning on my strength. Here is where I come back to Christ. I pray. I get to come to him boldly for mercy and grace, because that is what I need. That is what we all need.

Leading in Prayer

Heavenly Father, I am in awe of your lovingkindness, mercy, and grace. Thank you for sending the Holy Spirit to soften the rough edges around my heart. Forgive me for spewing harsh words and reacting with pride. As the opportunities arise to mature in the fruits of the Spirit, may I recognize it is you at work in me. I love you, Lord. Help me love others well. Amen.

"We must stay focused on who we serve. We often want to lead in strength but can forget the most significant strength when we lead others as Jesus led—with humility and kindness."

–Robyn Luftig

Multi-Award-Winning Author

CHAPTER 9

Shut the Should Down

Candace Payne

Internationally known as "Chewbacca Mom," Candace Payne became a viral sensation overnight. Her 2016 Facebook Live video shows her trying on a Chewbacca mask and holds the record for the most-viewed Facebook Live video in history (174+ million views). She has been featured in 3,000+ media outlets including *Good Morning America, The Late Late Show* with James Corden, The *New York Times, PEOPLE,* and *Cosmopolitan.* As author of *Laugh it Up, Defiant Joy, and Simple Joys,* she dispels the myth that joy is frivolous, or reserved for a few select "happy" people. Candace invites you to receive the freedom and joy God created for your life.

People call me a joy evangelist, but what's funny is that I did not come up with that phrase. After my Facebook post with the Chewbacca mask went viral, *Cosmopolitan* did a write-up, and that's what one of their editors called me—a joy evangelist, and I thought it was a perfect sentiment. Isn't that hilarious? Honestly, it was a long time coming to discover joy as my spiritual mantle. I feel my overarching desire is to see people live a life full of joy, expressing joy, feeling joy, and owning joy. There are a lot of facets that come underneath the big umbrella of joy. So that coined term, joy evangelist, felt like it was perfect for my actual calling in life.

> **"I have told you this so that my joy may be in you and that your joy may be complete" (John 15:11 NIV).**

Here's the misnomer about joy we're battling as Christian leaders. There is a belief we have to have hope in order to experience joy. And, somehow, we've got to pull up our bootstraps to get hope. There's a big mystery in this uncovering of being hopeful. I'm going to be honest with you, just like so many others throughout the pandemic; I've experienced a life that's left me hopeless. I'm dead serious. Just hopeless. And when I read this passage, Romans 5:3-5, it just blew my mind. "Not only that, but we rejoice in our sufferings knowing that suffering produces endurance, and endurance produces character, and character produces hope, and hope does not put us to shame, because God's love has been poured into our hearts through the Holy Spirit" (ESV).

The succession of these things hit me like a lightning bolt. I'm always trying to get my hopes up first, so I can then experience real joy. But this scripture tells us we encounter joy in our sufferings. We understand suffering produces endurance, endurance produces character, and then our character produces the hope we need at the right time. I have had the cart before the horse. I was trying to keep my hopes up in the middle of my suffering. But the Bible doesn't say to remain hopeful in the middle of your suffering. It says rejoice in your sufferings because you know it will lead you to hope. It will eventually lead to hope for better things. It's hard for a naysayer who is negative and always annoyed at the world to find hope. They haven't been able to accept hope because they don't recognize suffering as an opportunity for greater joy, hope, endurance, and character. In the midst of suffering, they don't see how one leads to the other.

The greatest feeling is knowing hope is the result of this process. Our character is built, and that's worth holding on to with both hands. Declaring this will make my outlook brighter. Amid your suffering, God will grow you. It takes a subtle shift in your thinking: This situation will not break me. This situation will build me.

Pause and Reflect

What is your first instinct when you're facing hardship? How has this reaction grown or made you feel defeated? In looking at a past moment of hardship or present circumstance, can you utilize the formula in Romans 5:3-5 to reframe your experience, embracing joy in all seasons of your life?

Just Stop It

In 2019, amidst writing and traveling, author and speaker Jenny Randle and I launched a podcast named "Shut the Should Up." It's all about finding freedom from everything we tell ourselves that we should or shouldn't do. We all have stuff put on us or that we pick up willingly that is not a part of our God-given identity. Through the podcast, we try to unravel the dogma and find the place where the Lord speaks through his Word, encouraging us to live authentically.

In this personal growth, I've just discovered and learned to understand new facets of my identity. God has made me a proverbial bull in a china shop just by the simple space I take up and carry when I walk into different places. For instance, I believe God called me to be a breaker and a builder within the Christian community. That's been difficult for me to realize because nobody, myself included, wants to come in and break stuff. Often, if God calls us to break something, we must recognize his desire to restore and build back up for his purposes. He's called me to bring attention to some things on the shelf. They're kept just for vanity's sake and nostalgia in the church, and they have no serving purpose. Yet, we're still clinging to those lifeless things.

I see the good in the church—the spots where she's thriving. But to look deeply at her, I must willingly take the time to see the reality of the church's wounds—the bruising others may not see. I know that there are certain situations God called me to address and say outright, "Hey, this is suffering here." We don't see and acknowledge what's tearing us inside out because we are too busy arguing about things that are unimportant—those things up on that shelf. We must be brave and obedient enough to say, "This stops here with us. Let's see how we can fix this."

We want to hear from God. We want a holy encounter, but it often appears too hard to get there. It's like the children of Israel when they saw the smoke, thunder, and lightning in the mountains that was the manifestation of God's presence. They wanted God's leading and provision, but they were intimidated and knew Moses would interact with him on their behalf. "Moses, can you go for us and talk to him or else we're going to die?" We need to be reminded that because of Christ's sacrifice, we can go to God personally. You don't have to wait for Instagram pastors to go into God's presence for you. You don't need another person to receive a word, package it in a lovely little meme, post, or an Instagram Live for you to digest secondhand. I want people to encounter a firsthand, real relationship with God because not only do we need it personally, but the world needs it. We don't need fluff from somebody else's encounters. We need our own personal time with God. He must be present in everything we do. So, I'm going to send out the challenge, rally the church and say, "Let's go."

Pause and Reflect

Can you describe a time when you felt it impossible to be your authentic self because of perceived unrealistic expectations of yourself or those around you? What are 3 steps you can take to liberate your heart and free your calling without these expectations. How can you create space for deeper personal encounters with God in your daily life? Examine any habits, traditions, or ways of thinking that don't serve God or his purpose for you.

Joy for the Long Haul

Sometimes we see God's call on our lives in the short-term mission trip mindset. It'll take a couple of weeks, and then it will end, wrapped up in a neat bow, and then we'll wonder, what's next? But I know that joy must always be a mantle for my whole life. I carry it as my mission. I won't see the end of this earthly work, and that's fine. I hope it goes that way for me. We hear the mandate go into all the world, and we're like, alright, well, how do I get there? It starts inside of you as an internal work of the Holy Spirit. Without the Holy Spirit's work, anything else you attempt to do is a vain pursuit—here one day and gone the next.

If God opens doors and allows situations to happen, you must be solid, and I mean this, rock solid in your identity in Christ and fully yielded to the Holy Spirit. We cannot walk in God's purpose for our lives, focusing on our human accomplishments.

I've seen what God put in me as a kid that said, yeah, moments are coming, but what do you do when all your dreams come true? What's the next step? Five years removed from the viral mask moment, I'm now seeing that wasn't the grandiose moment God had called me to—that was just an extra step in knowing the actual anointing I carry. I can help people experience joy.

Pause and Reflect

Can you list small moments in your life that have led to revealing your identity as a Christ-follower? How does this self-awareness empower you to recognize your calling? What are three tasks you can do to help you maintain joy through the journey of your life's work?

Leading in Prayer

Dear Heavenly Father, I thank you for helping me to embrace my authentic self. Deliver me from false expectations and powerless relics to which I have clung. I want to walk entirely in freedom and discovery as I embrace your joy in the journey ahead so others may see and experience it too. Let me take hold of every opportunity to operate in the fullness of your plan. Amen.

"Joy is strength."

-Mother Teresa

CHAPTER 10

FIND STRENGTH IN TELLING YOUR STORY

Sioni Rodriguez

Sioni Rodriguez's life is proof of the power of prayer to effect real transformation. Sioni was born in Mumbai, India, but she moved to Costa Rica with her mother and brother when she was five. As a young child, she was sold into human trafficking as a sexual slave, but God showed up.

Sioni serves as the senior administration service technician at one of the largest insurance companies in New Jersey. She is an ambassador for Project Rescue, fighting against human trafficking and human rights violations. Sioni, a prison chaplain, Angel Tree program coordinator, and team member for Its Time to Heal: Beyond Survival International Ministries, is passionate about changing lives. As the 2018 Beyond Me Award (Advanced Writers and Speakers Association) recipient, for her biography, *Three Times Sold*, Sioni shares her story to reach others with the healing hope and power of forgiveness found in Christ.

In my childhood home, my alcoholic parents mercilessly abused my younger brother and me in every way possible. At age nine, my mother did the unthinkable—she sold me to a brothel. I remember sitting in the brothel waiting and crying for my mother to return. In my mind, she would be right back, but she never came back. Later that day, I escaped when the brothel owner left the door open. I walked out to the street, right into the heart of San José, Costa Rica. A man passing by saw me alone and crying. He transported me on a two-and-a-half-hour journey back home—the only home I knew. My mother responded in anger, asking, "Why are you back? Why are you here?" As a child, I just knew I wanted to come home. She beat me severely, but she allowed me to stay.

Pause and Reflect

Are there parts of your personal story that include betrayal and harm from someone who should have protected you?

Love Called to Me

My mother, a heavy smoker, often sent me on errands. One afternoon when I was almost 12, she sent me to get cigarettes at the convenience store. Somewhere along that 30-minute walk, I heard a sound that reminded me of bells. The sound drew me to a house full of people having church. I walked in and asked to join them. I listened to the pastor talk about God's love for us. The people were very kind and showed me so much compassion. The pastor said, "If you want to accept Jesus Christ as your Lord and Savior, just raise your hand."

I jumped up and said, "Yes, I want to know him." I thought this Jesus I met would fix everything in my life right away. But that's not what happened. Instead, the sexual abuse continued daily. As a child, I tried to commit suicide several times. I was never successful and never understood why. As an adult, I realize it was not yet my time. The devil tried so many times to destroy me, but God had a purpose for my life.

Pause and Reflect

In what moments do you recall God showing up during a difficult or traumatic time of life? Take a moment to write down what you remember about your first encounters with Jesus.

Refusing to Doubt Him

A year later, my mother sold me a second time. She led me to believe I was going away to be a babysitter. Deep down inside, I knew exactly what was happening and could do nothing to stop it. Trapped in that second brothel for three unspeakable years, I was so broken. I had become an object, something to be used. But I often remembered the day I met Jesus and the peace I encountered in that house church. I recall telling the other girls, "I know God's going to take me out of this place."

"Sioni," they would ask, "how can you say God will take you out of this place? Look where we are." I had to agree with them, but, I knew my encounter with Jesus was real, and I had faith in him. After years of looking for an opportunity to escape, I jumped out of the kitchen window. I again returned to the only home I knew, only to find my mother had opened her own brothel.

Pause and Reflect

In thinking about a personal time where everything felt dark and hopeless, what did you do to hold on to the promise of God's faithfulness? How can you use situations like these, past and present, to be a source of encouragement to others?

No More Going Home

Eventually, an American man purchased me from my mother and forced me to become his wife. This was the third time I was sold as property. Being married to him didn't change the fact that he was cruel and abusive toward me. He returned to America without me, and I remained in Costa Rica. I had to wait four years for my green card and then I joined him. During the four years, my mother continued to prostitute me every chance she got. By age 21, I was on American soil. Within 6 months, my husband divorced and abandoned me with our two children—my toddler daughter and six-month-old son. I did not know what to do. There was no way to get back to Costa Rica. I had no money and no job. I did not speak English. I felt ashamed to admit this for years, but I had no choice but to turn to what I knew. I prostituted myself to feed my family during this time. When I looked at my children, I knew I wanted something different for our lives. I learned English by watching General Hospital and shortly after I got my driver's license. I began to envision new possibilities. Within four years, I was cleaning schools as a janitor. I started saving a little money. In 1995, I was able to buy my first home. It was simple and humble, but to me, it was incredible. Unfortunately, in a lapse of judgment, I allowed my ex-husband, who purchased me, to move back in with me. It was such a costly mistake. He physically and emotionally abused me.

Pause and Reflect

Have you ever felt backed into a corner with no perceivable solution? In trying to move forward, how did you handle the situation?

I decided to attend a local church. Church was precisely where God wanted me. It was there that I learned more about God's character and his purpose for my life. Although I felt cared for and loved by my church family, I didn't want to tell them about the ongoing abuse. They would ask me where all the bruises came from, and I would say I fell. One day, I became bold and shared. I asked a woman in the church for prayer. Realizing I could not stay with my ex-husband, I decided to get out of the situation and my life began to change.

In 2003, I found my kinsman redeemer—the godly, loving man I am married to now. He has loved my children as his own. I currently work for one of the largest insurance companies in New Jersey. I started in the mailroom, and God promoted me, through prayer, to one position after another. God helped me learn quickly as I remained faithful to him. I am now the senior administration service technician and I attribute all my success to God.

God has called me to speak life into women who are incarcerated and serving life sentences. I tell them that even in prison he can use them. He calls everyone to be used wherever they are.

He called Paul to lead in the prison so that others might know Christ. Even in the brothel, God gave me hope amid desperation. I am proof of God's goodness. He stays and sees us through the darkest situations of life. Because of his faithfulness, I want others to experience his freedom.

Pause and Reflect

Are there secrets in your life that keep you from moving forward in peace and freedom? What steps can you take to become transparent before God in these situations? How can you put boots on the path to transform your life?

How have you seen God work during your honest faith walk with him?

Transformational Conversations

Without a continual conversation with the Lord, I would be miserable, depressed, and living with no hope. Because I pray, my life is full of redemption and love. Prayer has softened me—it's helped me to love people and trust again. I believe if I had not prayed through all the trials in my life, I wouldn't be who I am today. Because of my difficult journey, I relate deeply to the women I mentor. In my intimate conversations with God, I have learned to forgive. We can pray as much as we want, but if we are unwilling to forgive, there is no forward motion. We're stuck and can't go anywhere. Sometimes we feel our prayers are unanswered and the wait is too long. God has rewarded me tremendously in the waiting. He tells my heart that he has all the details in place.

Pause and Reflect

Describe your conversational times with God. How do these moments compare with the conversations you have with people in your life? What do you receive in your moments with God?

Shamed No More

God uses the circumstances that have brought me shame to help others. This wasn't easy. But when God promotes, he gives a new level of confidence. You have potential because of Christ in you, and you were created with a purpose. When you feel disqualified by your past, you don't need to be overwhelmed with self-doubt. You don't have to kick down doors in your own strength. God will provide everything you need.

My prayer for you, my sister, as you abandon shame is to walk in great success and become who He's created you to be.

Leading in Prayer

Heavenly Father, I know you have a purpose for my life. You've called me and there's no mistake in this. Even in the darkest moments, you stay when others leave. I thank you for exchanging my shame for hope and new purpose. Although life may be difficult, I look for the light you provide at the end of the tunnel. When evil surrounded me, you made a way of escape. I praise you and choose to walk faithful to your plan. Amen.

"You may encounter many defeats, but you must not be defeated. In fact, it may be necessary to encounter the defeats, so you can know who you are, what you can rise from, how you can still come out of it."

-Maya Angelou

American Poet

A Letter to the Sisters Who "Aren't Finished Yet"

Precious Sister

You are unique, and God has gifted you with spiritual strengths and personal flair. God called you and placed his anointing touch and blessing on you. You even have credentials from schools of higher learning and the school of life. So why have you considered quitting?

Some complain, "I'm too busy." Others say, "I'm discouraged." Or burned out or just plain tired. When you are busy, get help, but don't quit. And if you feel burned out, search for a new flame to kindle the fire again, but don't settle for ashes. When you are tired, rest, but don't give up.

***

I co-own a publishing company. We opened the business because we felt an urgent directive from God. We produce quality books with powerful messages of God's love and salvation. Not to mention making opportunities for aspiring writers.

But there are days.

Moments when I want to close the doors and run as far away as possible. You too?

You may feel your life and your ministry is a failure, but God isn't finished with you. His hope lives in you even if you've stuffed it into a deep hole. Jesus didn't give up on Peter for sinking into the waters of unbelief. He did not terminate Martha because she washed dishes instead of sitting at his feet. John Mark abandoned Paul and Barnabas on a missionary trip. Anna was widowed 84 years. Rahab ran a house of prostitution. Yet God made a way for each person. To not give up. To continue to grow and press on (See Philippians 3:12 NKJV).

I worked more than thirty years for a major corporation and rose to the top executive ranks before we'd ever heard the words *glass ceiling*. I loved my job and the perks of upper management—travel, cars, expense accounts, and the potent feeling of leading.

One day, the foreign company who bought our corporation eliminated my job. I thought I'd die. But God showed me his strength, and I left the corporate world to find His plan. And what a magnificent ride it has been. I wouldn't go back for three times the salary.

When you think about quitting, take these steps instead. Ask God to pour His strength into you. Remember why you started—your why? Believe in your ability to adapt and learn. Look forward. Change your attitude. Remind yourself, "I'm not finished."

You are God's precious treasure. Even if your past is broken and you feel like a failure, He has more for you. God says, "I am the LORD, who opened a way through the waters, making a dry path through the sea" (Isaiah 43:16 NLT).

Get up, sister, get busy on God's to do list.

Karen Porter is an award-winning author, an international speaker, certified coach of writers and speakers, and a successful businesswoman. She is co-owner of Bold Vision Books, a traditional Christian publisher (boldvisionbooks.com). Karen lives in Texas with her husband George. Connect with Karen at karenporter.com.

CHAPTER 11

BUILD ON THE LEGACY BEHIND YOU

Jennifer Miller

Founder of JSM Diversity and multiple nonprofit endeavors, Jennifer Miller, is a south Florida native, a lifelong diversity and inclusion educator, and social justice advocate. Educated in Political Science and Global Studies, she has over a decade of experience leading diversity dialogues and helping human resource departments become more equitable and inclusive. Jennifer has a multitude of skill sets—Worship Leader (Life Church East Kansas City), Barista, Church Planter, Pastor's Wife, and mother to a beautiful blended family of seven.

One of the funniest moments I remember from childhood is realizing that everyone didn't have a drum set, keyboard, or microphone stand in their family room. I grew up around so much music. Singers, dancers, musicians, poets—everyone could do something, especially my grandma. She was the matriarch. A mother to 13 living children, 17 pregnancies total (at a time when an epidural wasn't a thing), and the wife of the great Bishop James Campbell, district overseer for the Southern Region of the Pentecostal Church of God.

My grandma was from the Bahamas, specifically Cat Island. She grew up with the beach all around, the 12th child and second girl. Her name was Sylvia after Silver and her older sister's name was Goldean, after Gold. She told me so many stories about those days. She rode horses on the beach and ate from the ocean daily. I admired everything about her. Who she was, and as an immigrant who migrated to the United States in her early twenties, everything she had become.

After school, she would wait for my brother and me to get off the bus and lead us to the wonderful garden of greens, corn, and herbs in her backyard. She made the simple seem sacred and stretched toast and butter and cans of Chef Boyardee across dozens of grandkids. She taught me how to scale fish, pick sea grapes, and dramatize stories and poems from her childhood on the islands. My grandmother has dementia now, but her glory days were incredible. Days I appreciated then and reminisce on now, as she slips back and forth into time.

Even with all the good I remember, there were items I didn't understand as a child. Her Bible was so tattered and torn, with elementary penmanship and words in cursive that seemed to take a lot of effort. I remember her long conversations on the phone that mostly included her affirming "mhm" and "yes, I understand." I remember the broken veins in her legs and large lumps from standing in the kitchen too long. And I will not soon forget her cries as she sat alone in the kitchen or her bedroom chair when she thought no one was around.

I remember a lot about my grandma, but even with all the glory, I recall how much I never wanted to be her. The Pastor's Wife. The Matriarch. The Mom. The Minister. It seemed like too many jobs, the underappreciated kind, and I didn't like that people didn't appreciate my grandma. She sacrificed to make lives brighter and better, even at her own expense. Her role to me was so sacred, so grand—it seemed far above me or anything I could do. Heavy, in a way I understood, even when I was younger.

Fast forward many years, and here I am. The Pastor's Wife. The Matriarch. The Minister. The Mom. I have too many jobs, you know, the underappreciated kind. I am a mother of seven, a business owner, a worship leader, and the pastor's wife, the most self-sacrificing job. The thoughts I used to wonder about my grandma, I now so greatly comprehend. I spend my days on the phone or entirely engaged in life-altering conversations, listening to friends in need, offering "mhm" and "yes, I understand." My legs ache from standing in the kitchen too long or cleaning before we host a group of friends.

I understand the cries of surrender. They are not all sad cries; sometimes they are "Yes, Lord" or "Help me put you first, Lord" sighs. I look back at my grandmother often, far away from home, and everything she knew, dying to self for something greater, something intangible but worth it.

Pause and Reflect

Who are you now? Who did you want to become? How did you run away from or smack into who God wanted you to be?

Reconstruction

My husband and I did not have a grandeur or glorious start. Sometimes when we retell our story, we try to make it sound better than it was. Honestly, we smacked right into each other, not literally, but figuratively. He was a wanna-be bad boy in college, and I was a wanna-be holier-than-thou Christian. All the best ingredients for a dysfunctional romance. We did have something, though, and that was desire. We were both looking for more. We were both empty and needing to be filled. In those first few years, we tried to fill that emptiness with each other and failed miserably. That's an entire book in and of itself.

God knew exactly what he was doing. He knew what we could become. He put us in the best position to see how many times and ways we came up empty and forced us, when removed from family and friends, to depend entirely on him.

When that happened, something shifted. I will always remember the conversation. We sat down to try to talk about the destructive path our marriage had taken. We were leading pastorally but failing personally to honor our home. As voices elevated and tensions grew, there was dead silence—a fork in the road. I can't recall who said it first, but we both agreed that we could no longer fake it to make it. We would give it everything we had or decide to let it go.

The next year was the worst year of my life. I cried more that year than I did my entire married life. We left our role as pastors, leaders, and teachers and became broken people under intense reconstruction with the Father. That year, my husband and I grew closer than ever, and we have been fighting fair ever since. That doesn't mean we don't have conflicts or moments when we say the worst things (still sin natured and full of self), but our recovery time is faster, and the scar tissue from the past is a reminder of where we never want to be again.

Before we could truly lead others in the faith, we had to learn to surrender. We needed to allow the Lord to be the Lord of our relationship. God reclaimed his place on the throne of our marriage. We learned to walk with the Lord again.

Pause and Reflect

What time in your life brought you the most pain but the most growth simultaneously? What did it take? What did you gain? What have you forgotten? How can you remember?

Becoming Me

When I was younger, people would ask what I wanted to do with my life when I got older. I'd say, "Help people." I didn't know how to do this, but I did not want to be a pastor's wife. I ran from the pastor's wife role so hard that if the guy I dated wanted to be in ministry, I'd break it off. Seriously, watching my grandma was a hard lesson about giving. Ministry required sacrifice, and as I previously outlined, I was pretty selfish and self-absorbed.

Don't get me wrong—I loved to lead. I was the first to raise my hand to sing solos, lead ministry initiatives, and Bible studies. It was the responsibility part that did not tickle my fancy. The thought of causing someone else to fail because of my lack of mindfulness kept me up at night. I wanted to live my life and be free to make mistakes (albeit some intentional mistakes) with no one watching.

The only problem was that it didn't work—no matter where I was or where I wanted to be. I could see and solve problems, give up my sleep to help people, and really care about supporting the church. No matter how far I ran, God was always there. It was like an episode of the Twilight Zone, where every door led to the same hall. No matter which door I chose I was leading people to live their lives for Jesus.

One day, my newly sanctified husband came home and said, “I think I want to go to ministry school.” We’re taught, over and over again, “Jesus loves me” and he does—Jesus loves us. He is calling us to obey him and love each other. I then began to realize the life I was living, we were living, was more about what God was doing with and through us.

When I let go of my vision for my life, and when I truly realized I was uniquely equipped and called to use my god-print to help his mission, I wanted to be more responsible, available, and surrendered. When I lost my life for his sake, I found it. Whether I am a barista (and I have been), a worship leader, a teacher, or an entrepreneur... I can do it all soberly minded for his glory.

I lost nothing when I became a pastor’s wife. The title is an occupation; that’s it. However, the occupation is a merit. It’s God saying, I trust you with this much more. I am so honored to serve our King this way. His glory is our purpose. His purpose is our mission. Our mission is our calling, and God’s calling on our lives is a job well done.

I am all I am because of who he is; every dinner, phone call, and meeting is worth it. It’s worth the glory of God. Besides, I have the best seat in the house for all the perks of living a surrendered life. I have the greatest CEO of all time, the creator of the world.

Pause and Reflect

What are you holding on to today? What area have you forbidden God to work in your life? Are you ready to surrender completely? If so, what steps can you take to move into surrender?

Leading in Prayer

Heavenly Father, thank you for the beautiful history you have allowed me to know. I am grateful for those that have gone before me, and I pray for those that come after me. You are so good to walk with me, surrounding me with people that help prepare me to use my gift for your glory. May your name, Jesus, be the legacy that is left by my life. Amen.

"If your actions create a legacy that inspires others to dream more, learn more, do more and become more, then, you are an excellent leader."

-Dolly Parton

County Music Recording Artist,
Actress & Philanthropist

CHAPTER 12

Get Out There

Martha Bolton

Emmy-nominated writer, author, and playwright Martha Bolton sums up the secret to success with one phrase: "Just let God use every gift you have." Her work as a staff writer has extended to many comedy greats, including the legendary Bob Hope. In 2021, she collaborated with Linda Hope to write the award-winning, top-selling book *Dear Bob...Bob Hope's Wartime Correspondence with the G.I.s of WWII.*

The highly acclaimed book was Christian Market Book of the Year (2021), Golden Scroll Memoir of the Year (2021), a 2022 Selah Award, and the 2021 Grand Prize for Military and Home Front category in the Chanticleer International Book Awards.

I was nine years old when I started writing. I still have the little books I wrote as a child. I wanted anyone who came over to read them. I was so excited about writing. Before I went to sleep every night, I would read the poetry I'd written that day. It is still one of my core memories. I couldn't wait to get up in the morning and write again. But since I was incredibly timid, I had a hard time being comfortable whenever the spotlight came my way.

One day, my creative writing teacher read one of my poems in front of the class. I hid in my usual spot in the back of the classroom in my chair, far away from everyone. There was a continual struggle—me wanting to get my writing out there with the tendency to shrink back, not wanting to attract too much attention. But when I entered a joke "gag writing" contest for the local newspaper, they printed my caption. I was ecstatic and took that as confirmation. No matter what, writing would be part of my future.

Humor was also a part of my growing-up years, which is why it became a big part of my writing. My parents were both funny during the most intense moments of crisis—I think that's where I got the same sense of humor. Just seconds before, we'd all be crying; they would say something funny, and laughter would erupt. As the youngest of five children, it was natural for me to offer something funny to break any stressful situation. It's true, laughter is good medicine, and God gave me the gift to use it. When someone was experiencing sadness or in a crisis, I would say something funny to lift their spirits, ease their pain, and bring a smile to their face. Sometimes, the only way to quell grief and stress was to say something funny. As I got older, I realized that helping people laugh was my purpose in life alongside writing, and I was going to use that for God.

When I became a church secretary, I never let myself lose sight of those gifts. Focusing on that purpose, I discovered a way to utilize writing and comedy in my job description. I started by writing a roast for pastors at my church. Before I knew it, word spread. Other churches called me to script a roast for their pastor. People started contacting me to roast their bosses too. It happened so organically. I didn't know how God would use this offbeat talent and orchestrate it all. Still, I was open to using my gift in any way he wanted and at any opportunity. Because of my willing heart, he did just that.

From the beginning, as I focused on using my gifts for God, it was important not to tear others down to get a laugh. In a society where making fun of others is the norm, I chose to say no to opportunities that compromised the boundaries I'd set. For example, although roasts can be funny, it's not a tribute if the guest of honor is not laughing. I learned what was safe by interviewing the honoree. Discovering what I could and couldn't talk about was important to me. I wanted to honor the person and stay within the boundaries of my convictions because it wasn't about just getting a laugh. I didn't know God would open doors to work in my giftings professionally outside the church world. That's how God surprises us with the unexpected—those bigger-than-life opportunities we wouldn't have if we weren't actively seeking to utilize our talents in whatever way it presents itself.

Pause and Reflect

If you could do one thing, whether or not you got paid, what would it be? Is there anything God might want you to dust off for kingdom purposes? Who are some like-minded people in your life or community that could help you as you move forward?

I took the leap and sent my material out to some of my favorite comedians of the time. It took a while to receive a reply, but Phyllis Diller was the first to say, "Yes." I started writing for her. Deep down inside, my dream was to write for Bob Hope. But he was a legend, and I was a church secretary. I decided script writing would be where I would start, so I went for it. Eventually, I met a gentleman, a staff writer, who also wrote for Phyllis Diller. He was the creative consultant for the television sitcom ***Mama's Family.*** One day, he invited me to come to the studio and watch a taping of the show. I brought my scrapbook with all the humorous newspaper column clippings and jokes I had previously written just in case an opportunity presented itself. I've learned the value of being prepared.

My husband came with me that day, and we all went to dinner after the taping. I must admit, I thought to myself, Now that I have him trapped in the restaurant booth, I can get him to look at my scrapbook. When he started looking through it, he said I should be writing for a television show. He recommended I write a script, and he would give it to his producer for review once completed. I told him I was down for the challenge. But I had one problem—I didn't own a working typewriter. I wasn't about to let that stop me. At the local library, I found the solution. There I could pay 25 cents to use their typewriter for 20 minutes. I fed this typewriter quarters like a slot machine in a casino. I may have spent more in quarters than our house payment for the month. I ended up writing not one script but two.

The producer read my scripts and asked me to pitch a few show ideas for the following season. As you can imagine, I was beside myself—so excited. Unfortunately, in Hollywood, many shows don't get picked up and at that point, ***Mama's Family*** was one of them. Naturally, I was beyond disappointed. But then, the producer suggested I try writing for Bob Hope. Talk about a full-circle moment—

it was a dream come true. I questioned myself. Could I do this? It was the opportunity of a lifetime, so I couldn't let doubt or fear hold me back. I took his advice, wrote a few jokes, settled back, and waited and waited and waited.

One evening, the phone rang around eleven o'clock. Coincidentally, a guy at my church did voice impersonations, so when the caller introduced himself as Bob Hope, I didn't believe him. I replied, "OK, Frank, I know this is you, and you're not even that good." But the joke was on me; it turned out to be the real Bob Hope. Talk about embarrassing. During our phone conversation, Bob told me he loved my work and gave me a few assignments.

Pause and Reflect

What do you find holds you back the most when focusing on your passion/purpose? Time? Resources? Motivation? Do you need help to figure out where to start?

Push Past Comfortable

Several projects later, I eventually became Bob's full-time staff writer. His first female staff writer of seven. When I started, this industry had more men than women, but this was my time. I was aware other women didn't get the same opportunities. To this day, I still consider it a privilege to be the first. The job also allowed me to balance life as a wife and mother. I could stay home with my children, take them to school, pick them up daily, chaperone field trips, and even serve as president of the PTA. I couldn't have asked for a better team to work with, either.

Surprisingly, the most significant glass ceiling I broke through was overcoming my shyness. I had a hard time speaking up, especially if it was a loud environment. I was timid and had to learn my lesson the hard way. Often, I'd be in the middle of a group of people collaborating and suddenly get a great idea. While mustering up the courage to share the concept whirling around in my head, someone else would speak up and say it first. "That's a brilliant idea," someone else would say. I wanted to kick myself for hesitating. Has this ever happened to you? You know, those "I told you so" moments when you get mad at yourself later. There have been many experiences like this over the years. I remember when there needed to be a line change, and we would have to go to Bob's dressing room and discuss these changes with him. It could be intimidating.

I owe my colleagues the world for pulling me out of my comfort zone rather than letting me hang in the background. During these dressing room meetings, we needed to think quickly on our feet and come up with lines right on the spot. Bob would be in his chair getting his make-up done. Seated around him were stars like Lucille Ball, Milton Berle, Danny Thomas, and so many great comedy legends. Each time I left his dressing room, I pinched myself. *Was this really where God's gift of humor had taken me?*

Pause and Reflect

Recall a time when you were afraid to speak up, share your voice, and contribute to a conversation. Why did you feel insecure about what you had to offer at the time? How can you change your thinking to help you step forward and push past your comfort zone?

Lessons in Influence

Bob was a wonderful boss. He never made me feel like I was less than in the workplace or not contributing as much as the guys. He was always compassionate, especially when he knew my kids were sick at home or if there was a family emergency—family always came before work. The thing I loved the most about Bob was that he was a class act in his comedy. Bob had moral boundaries and would never kick anyone when they were down. He was so respectful. It could be a worthy news story or a person going through a hard time, but he would never take circumstances like this lightly or make jokes at someone else's expense. We all learned a lot from Bob by watching how he lived his life.

This journey has helped me learn the importance of my voice. I realized that if I kept it inside, I wasn't doing anyone any good. Bob gave me confidence in my writing, propelling me to hone my gift. I also found out that many in this industry struggle with shyness, just like me. Even though I believed the opposite, these were my people. They struggled just like me. When I realized that, I understood I could help them find their voices as I did. I can help others see that shyness isn't a personality flaw, but an excellent God-created quality. Staying on my path and in my lane was my goal. Before I knew it, God promoted me—even past those who intentionally wanted to prevent me from moving forward. I had to trust him to open the right doors at the right time. If you had told me God would allow me to influence some of the rooms I've walked into throughout my lifetime, I would have laughed in disbelief. I will always be grateful for the opportunities he has given me.

Pause and Reflect

Is there someone who inspires you to lead with excellence? Write down some of the qualities they demonstrate that you admire most. How has their influence shaped you and your desire to grow?

Laugh Through it All

Jeremiah 29:11 is a verse that has encompassed not only my professional life but also my personal life. "'For I know the plans I have for you,' declares the Lord, 'plans to prosper you and not to harm you, plans to give you hope and a future'" (NIV). Even when things look bad or I struggle with disappointment, I never forget how God continues to be faithful to his plan for my life. He gives me writing ideas each day. Knowing whether things go as I want or if I lose the very thing I've prayed for—one thing is my constant—God, in his goodness, is working on my behalf all the time.

We will never understand the extent of how God is utilizing our gifts and our lives on this side of heaven. If we go through our days with a willingness to say, "God, here is all I have; use it," you will not miss out on having an impact. Sometimes I still must pinch myself when I think back to his faithfulness in every aspect of life. We've journeyed through many difficult circumstances—a stillbirth, miscarriage, then the adoption of two children, followed by the birth of our son. Our 22-year-old grandson, who is awaiting a kidney transplant and has a heart condition, recently had a truly miraculous recovery from a coding incident in the ER. He spent close to 30 minutes without a heartbeat. Is it any wonder that my motto is Life's hard, God's good, and laughter is calorie-free?

I have experienced the purpose of pain, and I can say God has been so good to me. He has blessed me with a far greater career and family than I deserve or sought out. And I am so thankful. For the good times, the hard times, and especially, the gift of laughter. I will always use it to find comedy in the chaos.

Leading in Prayer

Heavenly Father, thank you for the unique gifts that you've given me. Help me recognize and utilize them for your glory and purpose. When I lack confidence, remind me you are with me, you equip, and you have called me. Help me overcome the temptation to shrink back. Give me the courage to push through the uncomfortable places as you position me for what you have next. Amen.

"Whatever room I go into, I've learned to allow the Lord to step in first. And He's faithful. I don't have to worry about being the loudest or the smartest voice in the room—I will never be the smartest. But that never stops the Lord from using me."

-Rene Gutteridge

Award-Winning| Best-Selling Author & Screenwriter

CHAPTER 13

Don't Be Afraid of Small Beginnings

Deborah Maxey

Deborah Maxey's fascination with character and conflict was the driving force behind her career as a psychotherapist. She specialized in working with traumatized, abused, and neglected children and served as an expert witness in the courts. As an award-winning fine artist, her large oil canvases embrace photorealism.

Deborah is also an award-winning author. Her first novel, *The Endling*, includes artists and the art community. Having grown up with the teachings of Native American customs, Deborah's love for that culture has been lifelong. She is home in the Appalachian Mountains. The Appalachian people, their traditions, values, and way of life are a source of constant inspiration and creativity.

Go big or go home. Don't be average, be awesome. If you can't run with the big dogs, get back on the porch. You've got this.

But what if you don't? What if, in a world of people knocking their projects out of the park, you aren't even sure how to hold a bat? Even worse, you're wondering what in the world you are doing on the team. You don't know what to do, but you're willing to try because the coach is calling on you.

> **"Do not despise this small beginning, for the eyes of the Lord rejoice to see the work begin" (Zechariah 4:10 TLB).**

The hardest part of every beginning is knowing where to begin. Floundering around for the **Start Here** sign can be the first place we give up. We figure maybe it wasn't meant to be. We rethink our commitment, question if we were really called, stall, procrastinate, and, worst-case we back out.

Starting when we aren't sure of the outcome takes courage. Plain and simple.

When I was a child, my grandmother introduced me to the idea of a hope chest and gave me a pretty box to collect things for my future home and the role of wife and mother. Granny's hope chest was a large model made of cedar. But, because we moved so often (I attended 21 schools from first grade to high school graduation), mine was portable, the size of a shoebox.

I collected a few baubles and things I made, like potholders. I still have an ancient package of Kool-Aid in the box, a symbol that I wanted children to share it with someday. But by far, the most treasured items in the box are my letters to God.

The letters came about because I had no idea what to hope for or where to start. I did not have a healthy working model of marriage. My grandmother was widowed when I was five. That same year, my parents had the most spectacularly dysfunctional divorce ever.

Looking back now, I can see I started in the right place. I said, I don't know what to ask for, God, even though I didn't foresee his answer coming. He answered with an incredible Christian man I would marry (52 years and counting) and a joyous, fulfilling, love-filled life.

Because I grew up in poverty, I certainly didn't fill that box with hope for a grand wedding or fairy tale existence. I asked God for a mate that was a friend like the one I had in Jesus. I asked for someone that would commit to me, a friend I could talk to, lean on, and love while being loved in return.

All the while, when it came to the hope chest, I kept thinking sooner or later, I would know where to start. I didn't realize that my letters to Jesus were my first small start. I also didn't realize God was using my ability to admit, I don't know, to put me on a path to leadership.

Pause and Reflect

Is it hard to admit you don't know where to start? Can you recall when you sought God first because you had no clue where to begin? Did you have a mindset that kept you from talking to God in the first place? Pride? Fear? Opinions of others?

Those First Scary Steps

It would be unheard of now, but in all the nineteen new schools I attended after second grade, I checked myself into the school. Alone. The scariest part of every new semester was walking into a new building with an envelope that contained my grades and health records. As I left for those anxiety-filled first days of school, my mother's instructions were, "Just go to the office and hand them this."

Okay. But where is the office door? Trust me. They are not all at the front of the school. Once I handed off the documents, I soon learned to anticipate being met with the office staff's confused, compassionate, angry, or horrified looks. As they fought through their amazement and alarm, they peppered me with an onslaught of questions that filled me with shame, fear, and hurt. "Where is your parent? Why are you by yourself?"

These encounters taught me quickly that I would have to face some scary things to achieve a task. But I had a secret weapon. When I was saved at age six, Granny taught me Joshua 1:9."Be strong and courageous. Do not be afraid; do not be discouraged, for the Lord your God will be with you wherever you go" (NIV). Trust me, I took it literally, which the Bible intended.

I unwittingly reinforced Granny's lesson because as soon as we moved into a new house, on Sunday, I walked to the nearest church, no matter the denomination.

Again, with the doors. The sanctuary door is an easy find. But finding Sunday School was impossible. Once inside, I was always met with kind, loving, shocked Christian adults. They made sure I felt welcome. And while they asked many of the same questions as school officials, their hearts were in a different place. Instead of focusing on parental neglect, they saw my heart. The foundation of those churches gave me the courage to face each new school.

Behind every new door, folks looked at me like I was in the wrong place. But I knew God was ever-present with me. I thought of him as my personal portable God. He was inside me and no one could take him away. I reassured myself that the power of everyone around me didn't equal the power of God inside me. So, I persevered. The leadership skill that God was teaching me was perseverance. Even when I had no support, I recognized I was not alone.

Pause and Reflect

Do you persevere, even without the support of others? Does the idea of not being supported deter you? How can you shift your focus to move forward? What strengthens your perseverance?

Private Anchors

With every new church I attended, I had one goal. I would look for paintings that were anchors for me. Visuals that signaled to me I was home. The first was a picture of Jesus holding a little lamb. Hundreds of times, I imagined Jesus holding me like that—I knew he was my shepherd. He heard my voice. The other picture was of Jesus surrounded by children—like me. Once I connected with the pictures on the wall, peace settled over me.

New states and neighborhoods meant isolation. As an avid reader, books and characters became my friends. In every new school, I anxiously looked forward to finding the library. There, I would run my hands along the spines of my favorite books, where my friends lived. That was enough to ground me.

In the fifth grade, I received a wonderful gift. The Gideons came to my school to hand out little New Testaments. My heart sang. It was small enough to carry with me everywhere. Granny taught me that the living Spirit of God was in his Word. I took that literally, too, and carried that small Bible daily. God was instilling in me the value of emotional stabilization. I learned how to use my environment in difficult situations to allow his comfort and peace to flood me—a skill that would serve me for life.

Pause and Reflect

How do you foster emotional stability? What private anchors do you have—are there physical anchors that ground you? Perhaps a picture of your family, an award that guarantees you are not an imposter, a diploma that was difficult to finish? What assures you that you are his and he is yours? Maybe a cross, an angel pin, a David stone in your pocket?

Small Offerings

I was never sure I would find a way to fit in with each new church or school. But more than that, I wondered if anyone would see me there. I knew God gave me several talents. I could sing, draw and write. The ability to use those gifts was never assured with any new start.

My shabby clothes, and crooked home haircuts, were not a natural shoo-in for many activities that would allow me to be recognized. I knew I couldn't try out for glee club—no money for uniforms.

While reflecting on the Bible verses about not hiding my gifts under a bushel, my philosophy changed. It didn't matter what people thought. I would be moving along, and everyone around me would change in six months anyway. God had told me not to hide, so I sang along whenever the occasion arose, and those strangers recognized my gift.

I used my pencil to draw the teachers, the rooms, and the students. And because God gifted me with the ability to create a likeness (although I could not afford art supplies), that skill was acknowledged, too.

And I have always been a lover of words. A regular logophile. Words in the Bible, words in books, words of self-expression spilled out of me when there was no one to hear. Words spoke to, healed, and expressed my heart. I manipulated them until I was satisfied. With each new beginning, I was a nobody that wanted acceptance. It seemed my gifts would get recognized just before it was time to move again. I got positions working on the school newspaper, including anthologies, art displays, and solos in churches, only to leave them behind and start over. The dance was like a seesaw.

I committed to letting God handle if and how I was seen. Remembering that recognition, when I glorified him, validated his presence in me. Following the Bible, I didn't hide my talents. When asked to volunteer, I said yes and signed up to help. I learned to rest in his timing as he stretched my patience for acceptance into a leadership skill.

Pause and Reflect

How did you develop patience? What gifts and talents do you want to express? How can you go boldly before the Lord and ask him to utilize those gifts as he sees fit?

The Power to Push Through

Like Sisyphus in mythology, I built quite a muscle with every new beginning. Pushing that stone uphill made me strong.

All those new beginnings magnified my need for Jesus. He never let me down and trust developed. Then love, real love, for my portable Savior grew. Whenever I was tempted to feel sorry for myself for not having support or facing bullies (that's another story), I would reassure myself with my favorite phrase. My inner voice conveyed the audacity of anyone to mess with a child of the Most High God, by thinking, Really? Do you know who my Father is? That line has served me thousands of times.

And as my Granny would say, it helped make me as stubborn as a borrowed mule once I set my sights on something. God was creating tenacity in me. Tackling small beginnings, over and over without bitterness, anger, or resentment, built tenacity for all the other tasks he had for me.

Pause and Reflect

In what way do you see God building tenacity in you? How are you utilizing it to move forward in your leadership call?

All Together Now

I wish I could have whispered in that second grader's ear, "Deborah, you'll grow up to tackle incredible things. You will have a loving family, a successful career as a fine artist, and sing solos in large churches. You'll get a Ph.D. and have a thriving practice as a counselor, fearlessly facing court battles over a thousand times as an expert witness. You'll write, be published, and express your heart for others to read. But best of all, Deborah, you have Jesus in your heart, little one. And that, sweet child, is the key to every scary door you search for and open."

How awesome that God looks on us with joy when we begin. All because we are willing to start.

Leading in Prayer

Heavenly Father, When life picks me up from all that is familiar, and sets me back down to start all over again, I ask you to surround me with your presence. Remind me you are a constant companion, always ready to help me step out and embrace the next part of our journey. When I feel small, remind me that nothing you have called me to is insignificant. Thank you for your affirming guidance as I take each step into all you have for me. Amen.

"For one thing we know beyond all doubt. Nothing has ever been achieved by the person who says, 'It can't be done.'"

-Eleanor Roosevelt

Politician, Diplomat & Longest Serving First Lady of the U.S.

Precious Sister

God, our Father, is with you in every inhale and exhale. In his presence, you are secure. He holds you at the center of his heart and mind. His brilliance is in your skin—you're designed to be his spotlight. He has a divine plan for each of our lives. Yet, it is up to us to surrender to the one who can do more than we could ever imagine.

Seeing his dreams bloom in our lives starts with one three-lettered word—yes.

Yes, Father.

God, I might not know what's in store for my life, but you have my wholehearted yes.

As disciples of Jesus, we don't need to know the whole story all at once. Could you imagine knowing every nerve-wracking, scary, happy, and sad moment of your life and then anxiously waiting for them all to pass? Are you ready to step up courageously and say, "I am willing to go on this adventure, no matter where it leads. I'm eagerly awaiting what you have in store."

It might seem crazy to hear what God wants us to do—both in the big and small ways. One time, I was on my way to do an evangelistic program for children, and the Lord prompted me to braid my hair. I know. It sounds so weird that God would be interested in my hairstyle. So I complied halfway—braiding the top half and leaving the length down. As the activities continued, I realized my braids weren't holding up so well. Then I did what I should have done all along and braided my hair into one long ponytail. A young girl who admired my new braid asked me to fix her hair, too. As we sat together during ministry time, the little girl started crying. I prayed, Lord, give me the words to minister to her.

He told me, "Tell her she is important." His words through me transformed her that day.

His words are for you too. He wants to show you just how important you are to him and his kingdom.

Perhaps words spoken over you made you forget your importance to him and his plans. The enemy has told you, through yourself and others, you have nothing to give. He has said you are not enough, and you need to be more like so and so. These words paralyze you from moving forward. It's time to break these lies off you by declaring the truth of God.

If we are serious about saying ***yes*** to Jesus, we must be willing to allow the Holy Spirit to do the reprogramming. A reprogramming of our thoughts and hearts. To walk, surrendering to the wholehearted, yes, our hearts must first be submitted to Christ.

Are you committed to saying yes even if everyone leaves your side and you are the only one left in the room? It's a commitment to be bold about your faith and to lead others to the One leading you. It's a commitment to respond with quick obedience when the Holy Spirit speaks. Honestly, this is a commitment to an abundant life.

God is telling you to rise to your appointed place in his kingdom—walk, talk, and live like children of the light wherever you find yourself. It may be as simple as following the Holy Spirit's nudge to put a braid in your hair, which leads you to someone in desperate need of encouragement.

Your Heavenly Father is speaking to you today. "Daughter, I want to use you as my vessel." He longs to talk to you, and he longs to hear from you. He has a dream for your life and longs to walk beside you in that dream—together.

You have so much to give to the world. His spiritual gifts are in your hands—use them. Ask God for supernatural boldness and walk in the truths of who he says you are. The time to live courageously is now.

Bella Wellborn is a missionary kid, worship leader, and speaker who grew up in El Salvador and Argentina, working beside her parents, Jonathan and Michelle, and siblings Alexis and Joshua. She plays piano and guitar and travels with her mother, leading worship with Kings Castle and Club Castillo Ministries. Bella has ministered in over 20 countries around the world. While continuing ministry in Argentina, she takes online classes at Southwestern Assemblies of God University (Waxahachie, Texas).

CHAPTER 14

Keep Love in Focus

Rosalind Li

Rosalind Li, General Manager of Dela Chambre Hotel in Metro Manila, Philippines, is more than a businesswoman. Her heart, to be the hands and feet of Christ, shapes everything she does. She realizes a significant part of her purpose in leading her team is to share God's love. Her faith is at the forefront of how she conducts business—staff member training, coaching, and directing the company's daily operations. Rosalind wants you to know that in sharing God's love in everything you do, you hold one of the most significant leadership roles you can ever have.

All my life, God has given me the desire to care for people. My father left us when we were young. Even though he didn't know the Lord, I have the privilege of being a third-generation Christian. My mother is a Christian and has been a successful businesswoman for many years. I learned a lot as I observed how she ran her business. As one of her primary caregivers, I continue to learn from her today. Witnessing her strength and faith has profoundly shaped my life. I always knew whatever I did personally and professionally, I wanted to take every opportunity to show people the love of Christ. That desire has enhanced the heart of who I am as a leader.

Pause and Reflect

How do you define strength in leadership? What specific strengths do you see in yourself? Consider how you can activate and utilize those strengths in your life.

Rethinking the Call

Initially, I went to school and received my bachelor's degree in nursing. However, there was a hotel management training event in Taiwan, where I was staying after graduation. My mother encouraged me to try it out. Even though this career shift was unexpected at the time, I enjoyed it. I realized a profession in the hotel industry, like nursing, allowed me to care for people and share the love of Christ. God's favor was with me, as I was quickly promoted to higher positions in all the hotels I served. Now, as General Manager of Dela Chambre Hotel, a prominent hotel in Metro Manilla, Philippines, I lead a team of 30 people.

Throughout my life, I have been driven to be excellent at what I do. As a Christian, I want everything to bring glory and honor to God. Reliability, trustworthiness, good management, and interpersonal skills are an important part of my life. But they aren't just for my boss or the guests who stay with us. I want my staff to know I value them for more than what they do. Even though I must ensure work gets done properly, I want our team to feel appreciated. I genuinely care for and love them all. Even if they make a mistake, we can use it as a lesson to help us all improve and grow. I consider them family—my responsibility to them is something I do not take lightly.

God calls us to love others the way he loves us—with sacrificial love so they might come to know him. Ephesians 5:1-2 holds tremendous significance to my life. "Follow God's example, therefore, as dearly loved children and walk in the way of love, just as Christ loved us and gave himself up for us as a fragrant offering and sacrifice to God" (NIV). That is a part of every one of our job descriptions as his children—it's our assignment to carry out.

Pause and Reflect

Is it difficult for you to establish meaningful connections with those you come in contact with every day? What are some of your most significant relational hurdles? List a few ways to mindfully show God's love in your interactions with others.

Resilience in the Face of Fear

Before the pandemic, our hotel occupancy was very high, especially in December and Chinese New Year. When the pandemic came, I immediately heard the news from my brother, "The country is going into a lockdown, and you have to close the hotel."

I called my team leaders and supervisor and announced, "We must close down the hotel today." Of course, everyone was scared. Because of Covid, I had to make a hard decision as I wanted them to be safe. I told them, "I don't want you to be afraid because the Lord is with all of us. And one day, we will be back." The staff returned to their homes. I stayed in the hotel for a while and checked everything before returning home. When the hotel didn't have income during the pandemic, I wanted to look after my employees. I knew not having work would be hard for them, so I talked to the chairman. We could give them groceries through the first few months, including food and rice. They were so happy.

Pause and Reflect

Have you ever utilized your influence and resources to support others in need? In what small ways can you intentionally shift your focus to care for others?

Redefining Your Role

Despite the hotel staying closed for two years, I knew it was essential to stay connected with my staff and let them know I was there for them. I called and had Zoom check-ins with them. I wanted to make sure they were doing ok and for them to see that I was available whenever they needed me. Although I never forced my beliefs on anyone, I did my best to encourage and pray with them when they were struggling. I genuinely wanted to know what was going on in their lives and how they coped from week to week. Whether or not they are believers, they need to know they are loved, valued, and missed. For some, these opportunities are the only way most people hear about or encounter God's love.

During those times, I would continually hear, "Ma'am Rose, are you going to open Dela Chambre again?" I knew it was essential to be strong for them because I wanted to be a good leader. My heart is always to share the truth and not hide from reality. But I also desire to protect my staff, just like the Good Shepherd protects me. Because of God's grace in my life, that is who I hope to be. No matter the fear I felt during this crisis, leading my team meant I had a job to do when no one could even come to work. No matter how bleak things felt, I continued to share God's promises, confident that he would bring us back together again. I regularly shared Isaiah 41:10. "So do not fear. For I am with you; do not be dismayed, I am your God. I will strengthen you and help you; I will uphold you with my righteous right hand" (NIV). This scripture continually gave me hope.

Pause and Reflect

Is it challenging for you to share your faith and the truth when the opportunity arises? If so, why? Identify scripture that would help support you in sharing encouragement more often.

Love That Transforms Relationships

I'm happy knowing my team saw that God is faithful. The Dela Chambre is open, and all the staff I had before have returned. One day, my team members told me, "We're not leaving anyone behind because this is family." We are very thankful because God heard our prayer. Dela Chambre is a family hotel. I want every guest to know that at our hotel, they can experience the love of Christ. When guests return to Manila, we want them to feel this is more than a hotel; it is their second home.

One of the essentials to building a sense of family within your work environment is to make God's love evident. As you love like Jesus, it will naturally draw people to you and they will see a difference in your life. Even in the most stressful situations when we feared our future, I could speak truth into our circumstances. Remember, God says, he will take care of his children because he loves us. We can be sure of that. We want others to know that too, so they know he loves them the same way. When people know they are loved and welcomed to the work-family table, they experience genuine hospitality.

Leading in Prayer

Heavenly Father, thank you for every opportunity you've given me to be your hands and feet. Help me discover new ways to serve those who serve with me. Give me sensitivity to the needs of people so they might experience your love. Allow my life to be a witness of your compassionate truth. Give me new and unique ways to show people how good you are and how much you care for them. Amen.

"True happiness. . . is not attained through self-gratification but through fidelity to a worthy purpose."

–Helen Keller

Author & Disability Rights Advocate

CHAPTER 15

Focus on the Essentials

Nancy Bogart

When Nancy Bogart decided to cook up a batch of lotion bars in her kitchen, she had no idea how God would use this endeavor to change her life, as well as the lives of thousands of others. Business exploded quickly, creating an opportunity for Nancy to help others earn an income for their families.

Jordan Essentials is currently a multi-million-dollar corporation, going well beyond the popular lotion bars, and has been featured on The Today Show. Nancy's heart, to lead from a place of faith and humility, has evolved into a community-oriented company to which people are drawn.

My story begins with my desire to be a stay-at-home mom. Being a family of five supported by one income made this a difficult task. I had to get creative and find a way to make some extra money without punching a time clock.

My background is in food science and catering, and I have a passion for creating recipes, but food spoils. After reading a book about the ingenuity of pioneer women, I was inspired to create something homemade. I created a solid lotion bar with ingredients that are good for the skin. Instead of using an ingredient from days gone by like lard, I used beeswax with Vitamin E. I blended the mixture with some oils and poured it into a soap mold. To date, we have made over 5 million lotion bars by using a very similar formula.

We began selling the bars at local school vendor events. My mother, who had a background in sales as the first female car dealer in the St. Louis area, urged me to put the product into people's hands. God gave my mom a boisterous personality, which helped our mission. People flocked to us. We recognized the opportunity to create the home-based business I'd been praying about.

I had met some women through Mothers of Preschoolers (MOPS) whose circumstances seemed similar to my own. We were all budgeting every penny and clipping coupons. I created a direct sales company. In this way, I could help friends and others without placing a product in retail stores.

The company, originally named Country Bunny, quickly grew in the first five years, and we sensed the market calling for a name better aligned with a serious direct sales skincare company. Jordan Essentials evokes the healing waters of the Jordan River. The river reminds us of the Promised Land, and it's where Jesus was baptized. Its waters flow into the Dead Sea, where nothing lives, and yet it's the most life-giving water. This company has been a resurrection miracle that God has done for our family and so many other families.

Pause and Reflect

Are there ideas, thoughts, and dreams that you haven't acted upon? What are they? What holds you back from grasping those creative reins and putting things into motion?

Growing through Change

My husband, Ron, believed in me more than I believed in myself. He is the smartest business person I know, and he managed the company for the first five years. When the recession hit, he said, "God called you to this business, but He called me to feed our family. I'm going to get a job. You're going to be okay." That change was an interesting part of God's plan for me as a woman in leadership. Ron is still on the board, but he stepped back and it allowed me to step into place and truly run my company.

I struggled for quite a while, but that's where faith comes in—and my God-given abilities. People could easily see how Ron had the skills to lead the company. However, I believe watching me run things and realizing the leap of faith I took to stand in that position inspires other women. I lead with compassion and empathy. I care about our staff members and consultants. I want people to do well. As a woman, I probably budget more conservatively. For our consultants and other women to see me lead this company with my husband's support is important. As soon as Ron stepped back and I stepped up, God released a supernatural grace and provision upon our business.

Pause and Reflect

Do you let other people do the hard stuff because you feel you aren't up to the task? In what ways do you think you fall short? Is there something you can do to overcome what you are lacking? Do you need education, training, resources, etc.? How can you move past feelings of inadequacy and embrace God's plan for you?

God Makes a Way

God has shown up in interesting ways. Early in the business, we would print a bunny clip art on the labels for the lotion bars. We printed them on my home printer, and my dad was my computer guy. At one point, he had taken my hard drive and then left for a cruise. I had orders coming in and had no way to print my labels. My husband suggested we pray, which we did, and then he went to the store to get printer ink. He came back with a recovery program and said, "I don't know if this will work, but let's try it." I plugged in the program and my bunny label was there. It was like God said, I'll always provide for you. Twenty-two years later, when challenges arise, I always think of that little bunny. Faith has carried us through.

Pause and Reflect

How do you respond when you can't think of a way to resolve a situation? Do you stress out, get mad, give up, or get busy? List active ways to continue moving forward in faith when things appear to be melting down. Select a scripture that will keep you grounded in faith when resolution is nowhere in sight.

Thinking Beyond the Pebble

In my leadership experience, I have learned the importance of going from me to we. The we mentality widens the focus beyond my own concerns and asks, "How does this affect us?" It reminds me of a simple pebble and the ripple that pebble will create when thrown in the water. I am not the only one affected by my decisions. It is something I've had to learn over time. I used to lament over the inability to see what is going to happen in the bigger picture. The we mentality helps me work through every possible scenario, even the mistakes. We adapt, adjust, and overcome.

A leader needs to be okay with admitting, I absolutely failed that right there. I can see it now. The deeper questions we should ask are: How do we deal with the situation? Who needs to own it? How do we let it go? And how do we move forward from it as quickly as possible?

I want to learn my lesson with a high level of ownership. People have a tendency to gloss over their missteps to appear infallible. I've discovered humility is integral to leadership. Leading authentically with humility allows people to feel safe and creates a healthy work environment. As a leader, I have learned to protect the workplace like I protect my home. I strive to create the same community and culture in both spaces.

Pause and Reflect

How hard is it for you to own your own mistakes? Create a short list of how you can mindfully shift from the ***me*** to ***we*** mentality. Do you have a pebble within your reach? How can you create a ripple of positive change for those around you? Can you envision how far that ripple could go—what would it look like?

Choosing a Better Life for Yourself and Others

At an event I attended, Doris Christopher, with Pampered Chef told me, "You'll find a fork in the road. Is it going to be people or is it going to be operations?" I have always been on the people side. My degree is in Hospitality

Management, and I enjoy inspiring people and creating great experiences for them. I love working with people, especially with women, even though I have three sons.

Not only has God abundantly–blessed my family through Jordan Essentials but so many other families as well. I have heard stories about husbands who were unemployed for a season and the Jordan Essentials business made the house payment. It covered college tuition. It has provided for families whose hot water heater has gone out, whose van has needed new tires, vacations, and so much more. For our family, the first big item Jordan Essentials paid for in the first two years was for us to go to Russia and adopt our daughter. We would not have had the time and resources to bring our daughter home and integrate her into our family had we not started the business. Our boys are better people because of their sister, who they love unconditionally, though she is quite different from them.

These life-changing experiences drive me to help people find the potential within to pursue their passion and find a livelihood through this business. I love helping people see the best of their God-given talents. It's an honor to pull back the curtain to reveal something that was already there. Sales can be hard. I watch women crushed with rejection when people say no, then get back up again. When the next person says yes, the confidence builds because they can see the potential, and their behavior begins to change.

This home-grown business serves people at different levels. It can be a great supplement for the person whose passion doesn't pay enough, the retiree who still needs to bring in an income, or the corporate worker who wants to add something fun to life. A friend of mine was struggling with the idea of making money and promoting. She was confusing poverty with humility. I said, "God wants his girls to have money so we can do good things." The real dream is not simply to make money selling healthy products, but it provides the ability for someone to spend more time with family or to do anything they can envision.

Pause and Reflect

Have you ever thought about how stepping into your calling might change the lives of others? What does walking in faith reveal about your gifts? How can you grow your gifts into something that thrives?

Leading in Prayer

Heavenly Father, help me step out in faith, take the risk, as I'm empowered by the gifts you've given me. Show me how to embrace change, be creative in my approach to problem solving, and envision the unique ripple my calling will cause in the world. Help me consider how my steps of faith might empower the lives of others. Let me walk in humility as you blow the doors open on this journey. Amen.

"In America, the mindset is to strive, strive, strive. But, when you strip it all down, success looks like following through with the call that God places on your life no matter what that looks like..."

-Lauren Daigle

Multi-Award-Winning
Recording Artist

CHAPTER 16

Refuse to Be the Mean Girl

Kerri Pomarolli

As a former recurring character on soaps (*Port Charles, Young and the Restless,*) and in movies, Kerri Pomarolli attracted industry big hitters. Coming to Hollywood, she found that compromising her faith was not worth the possible cost. God had other plans for her in stand-up comedy. Her first gig was at the world-famous Hollywood Improv in front of a secular crowd. Since then, Kerri has become one of Hollywood's biggest Christian spokespersons and recently voted one of LA's Most Inspiring People by *LA Voyage* Magazine.

A national headliner working with icons (Jay Leno, Jim Carey, Carol Channing and Jerry Lewis) Kerri is passionate about her faith. Kerri's latest two books, *Confessions of a Proverbs 32 Woman*, and *Devotions for the Proverbs 32 Woman are Amazon bestsellers.*

As a mom of two daughters and a former teenager, I have dealt with my fair share of mean girls. I went to a Dutch Reformed Christian school in the middle of Detroit. I didn't blend in well as an Italian girl that attended Catholic Mass. In my childhood, I rode on buses filled with gaggles of inner-city kids and was subjected to many mean-spirited "yo-mama" jokes. As a result, I learned to spar verbally. This way of life surrounded me.

When people learn to spar verbally with someone, they are introduced to the mean girl mentality. They learn that to defend themselves, they must be mean to others and make jokes at other people's expense. I was a part of this experience on both the receiving and giving ends.

I have always heard, "You don't become a comedian by being a cheerleader." I clawed my way to acceptance, always two steps away from the popular table. I tried hard to fit into a box that wasn't meant for me, and it caused so much grief. That is why it's important to talk with my daughters about acceptance and popularity. I tell them they don't need to fit into this world. I spiritualize these conversations, which often gets on their nerves. I have the conversations anyway because there are spiritual components to the battle for acceptance.

Pause and Reflect

Can you recall times when you felt like an outsider trying to be noticed? In what ways did you strive to fit in? Do you still battle with the effects of the mean girl mentality? What sacrifices have you made for acceptance? Have you inflicted harm on others by being a mean girl?

Ignore the World. Step Into God's Call.

As we strive for acceptance, we often conform to a mold outside God's plan. God has designed us to fulfill his purpose. He spent time crafting you into who you are—personality and all. He has done that with every human on earth. Why should we change to fit the standards of a society that harms and makes us the brunt of their jokes?

God has given each of us a significant calling. It took me a long time to find out what my calling was. I experimented with many different ideas, but God kept bringing me back to comedy. He gave me a platform to entertain people in a way that brings him honor. This is not to say that comedy came easily to me. I attempted to take two comedy classes and quit them both. I tried improv groups and other avenues before God opened the door to stand-up comedy.

Pause and Reflect

Have you ever felt God had a specific plan for you and your unique gifts? What are the steps you've taken to walk out that plan? What characteristics do you recognize God building in you for his purpose? Can you recall feeling pressured to assume a role to which you know God did not call you? How did you respond?

Reject Competition & Comparison

When you constantly compare yourself to someone who may have a similar calling, you allow yourself to become dangerously competitive. Thoughts enter your mind like I am not doing as well as they are doing. This negative self-talk leads to bitterness and deeply rooted dissatisfaction. It robs us of the contentment of walking in our God-given call. When you are unsatisfied with your calling, you can become a mean-spirited person. You may find yourself lashing out at others. This attitude can affect how deeply we allow God to move in our lives.

Sometimes we believe we deserve that big platform or sphere of influence. We become indignant and frustrated when it doesn't happen for us. We need to recognize this pride at its root. If pride is allowed to grow and remain unchecked, you will become the mean girl.

Even today, I struggle with comparing myself to other comedians. I compare myself to random TikTok videos on the internet. For example, I watched the video of the lady wearing the Chewbacca mask in her car cracking jokes. I have watched people shove cinnamon down their throats and get millions of likes and views. When I compare my audience reach to the crazy number of views their videos receive, I feel defeated. At that moment, I must assess myself and what spirit I'm allowing to influence me. I go to God and repent. God has me where I am without having to shove cinnamon down my throat or joke at other people's expense.

Pause and Reflect

Recall a time when you have compared yourself or your calling to someone else. How did you overcome this self-inflicted comparison? Describe the God-grown goodness he has placed in you to fulfill your call. What three steps can you take to walk in your call without competing with others?

Stomp Out the Spirit of Rejection

The enemy would like me to walk in a spirit of rejection. His tactics can lead me to reject the idea that I'm divinely called to serve a specific purpose. He tells me I am not good enough and I can't impact the Kingdom of heaven. Satan uses others to ignite my self-doubt. Phrases like you can't do that, you're not a good enough mother, or you won't succeed come to mind and can seep into my heart.

You do not have to allow negative or positive criticism to crush you. You do not have to live based on the words others say to you. Mean words do not define who you are. Christ himself bought you. God sent his Son to the cross so you might live and have the power to overcome self-doubt and hurtful words. Your Creator loves you and thinks you are worth more than the moon and stars in the sky.

> **"Even before he made the world, God loved us and chose us in Christ to be holy and without fault in his eyes. God decided in advance to adopt us into his own family by bringing us to himself through Jesus Christ. This is what he wanted to do, and it gave him great pleasure" (Ephesians 1:4-6 NLT).**

Pause and Reflect

What thoughts of self-doubt come to mind most often? Can you identify the source of that negativity? What three things can you do to shut down those voices and create healthy God-confidence? Choose a scripture to counterbalance negative thoughts when they invade your mind.

Leading in Prayer

Heavenly Father, help me look to you, not others, for guidance, grace, and acceptance. Forgive me when I have allowed comparison and competition to cause me to become the mean girl. Help me apologize and seek forgiveness from those I have harmed with my cruelty. I ask you to free me from the negative thoughts. Help me be strong, courageous, and confident in the calling you have placed on my life. Thank you for utilizing all my unique gifts for your glory. Amen.

"I don't have any time to stay up all night worrying about what someone who doesn't love me has to say about me."

-Viola Davis

Actress

A Letter To the Sisters Who Feel "I Am Alone in This"

Precious Sister

You are not alone.

You may be tempted to think you're on your own. You are probably tired of toiling away without support, cheering yourself on, and enduring storm after storm by yourself. Maybe you feel invisible. Nobody seems to care about your story or your struggles.

I know how you feel. When I moved from India to the U.S., I left behind all my near and dear ones. My husband was the only friend I had for miles. When I walked on the streets, my foreignness screamed, You don't belong.

But I do belong. God reminded me that even though I had no family or friends near me, I was never alone because he was with me and I belonged to him.

You belong to God. God chose and saved you so that he could dwell with and in you. Jesus sacrificed his life so he could make you his (1 Corinthians 6:19-20).

You belong to God's family. Your Father has gifted you spiritual siblings who are also co-workers chasing after the same purpose of magnifying God (Ephesians 2:19, 1 Thessalonians 3:2).

You are not alone in your calling.

Jesus' last command to his followers to spread the gospel to the ends of the world came with a promise that his presence would be with them everywhere they went (Matthew 28:19-20). You can take Jesus at his word. Even in the wilderness, when you feel afraid, isolated, or exhausted, you can trust the Good Shepherd to carry you on his shoulders.

You are not alone in your ministry.

As a writer who spends many solo hours on my computer, I need constant reminders that I'm not working in solitude. I can rely on the Holy Spirit sent to help me.

> "And I will ask the Father, and he will give you another advocate to help you and be with you forever—the Spirit of truth. The world cannot accept him, because it neither sees him nor knows him. But you know him, for he lives with you and will be in you" (John 14:16-17 NIV).

When you are prompted to think you're alone, stand firm on God's unswerving faithfulness. Believe that the Father has your hand in his and he will never let go. You are never alone.

Mabel Ninan (mabelninan.com) is author of *Far from Home* and podcast host of I*mmigrant Faith Stories.*

CHAPTER 17

Be Determined to Make a Lasting Difference

Tonquise "TQ" Evans

For Tonquise"TQ" Evans, hard work and intentionality are magnified by a fearless heart focused on reflecting the Fruits of the Spirit. As head of Chief Diversity Officer for the People Operations arm of Mediavine, a Florida-based marketing agency for content creators, TQ's mission influenced a company culture of kindness and diversity, both internally and externally. TQ's spirit shaped her life as an entrepreneur and designer of Prende pants, a birth doula, a devoted wife, and a mother to four kids. Her accelerated drive and determination focused on making every day count.

I want to introduce you to a trailblazer and one of the most fearless women I've ever known to grace this planet—my sister—TQ. You may not have thought about it before, but you can be the most significant positive influence in your sibling's life. That was my sister's impact on me. As a result of a long, resilient battle with cancer, TQ now walks in paradise. But I'll never forget one of the most powerful requests she made of me. "Nia, tell my story."

Sharing the stories of world-changers like my sister is one of the most incredible gifts we can pass on to the next generation. I want to give you a peek into the intimate, life-altering experiences that helped shape and mold me into the woman and leader I am today. My deepest hope is that TQ's life and legacy will continue to transform and inspire future generations. Let me walk you through a few of her life's well-lived moments—up close and personal.

Move in Confidence—Unapologetically

Growing up, my sister displayed immense courage and confidence, which I've always admired. She was bold, resilient, and walked to the beat of her own drum. TQ had the type of personality and confidence most people wished they had. She never concerned herself with what others thought of her and did whatever she wanted unapologetically. This level of tenacity would take most people years to obtain, but TQ had it naturally. It was just something about her. No one could quite figure out what that something was, but they wanted to know her better. Her spirit was infectious, and it impacted everyone she met.

One memory I can recall quite vividly. It was a significant turning point in my sister's early years. I consider this stage the transformation. TQ's journey toward self-discovery revealed the beginning of something much bigger than we could've ever imagined, and it all started with hair.

My sister's hair was naturally thick and very long. I always adored this because it was the opposite of mine, which was naturally soft and curly and only grew slightly past my shoulders. In high school, TQ was a trendsetter. As a reflection of her colorful spirit and personality, she would often perm and dye her hair in various colors. This wasn't uncommon for a teenager living in Atlanta, Georgia, in the mid-'90s. Because of the frequent exposure to chemicals used in perms and dye, TQ's hair became severely damaged.

One particular day, my mother and I were busy cleaning and completing chores around the house. TQ went into the restroom to get ready for the day. Shortly afterward, she stormed out of the bathroom toward my mom and screamed, "Look at my hair! It's so thin." She gently pulled her hair to show the severity of the damage. The more she pulled, the more hair came out into her hands. It shocked my mother and me to see how damaged her hair had become, and TQ began to cry.

Immediately, she dried her tears and ran back into the restroom. After a few hours, she returned to the kitchen with her hair cut off and shaved low. Seeing such a drastic change in my sister's appearance, my mother and I were more shocked than the first time she came out of the restroom. TQ spun around to show off her new look, then said, "What do you think?" Mom stood with her mouth open, baffled by this extreme transformation.

Her face softened, then she smiled and said, "It looks good on you. I'll take you to the barbershop so they can clean it up and make it look neat."

TQ wore her new look with so much confidence. She was a cheerleader in high school but didn't let how her squad might react to her new haircut deter her from this decision. It is almost like she tapped into an awareness of self and never looked back. It was an honor to witness this resilience up close. I pray we all find this level of freedom in the identity of our Creator. May we live a life free of restraints, fear, and judgment from others and be who God created us to be.

Pause and Reflect

What personal setbacks have you had to power through? Do you have a hard time dealing with life's curveballs? How can you become more self-aware and make the most of a discouraging situation?

Invest in Your Talents and Water What You Love Doing

TQ's confidence, natural talent, and resilience combined with something extraordinary. My sister was always passionate about acting, so she took drama classes at North Atlanta High School, known for its top-notch theater department. It was an ideal place to start if you were interested in becoming an actor, singer, artist, dancer, or musician. Admittedly, talents in the fine arts runs in our family. Our father is a skilled artist who can sketch landscapes and portraits, and I, too, can draw, paint, and recreate almost anything. Our Uncle L was an accomplished actor who played in movies and television. The acting bug had bitten TQ as well. Becoming an actress was one of her most impactful decisions.

Pause and Reflect

What are your interests? Are you naturally drawn to the arts, gardening, design, volunteering, or something else? How can you invest in developing your talents?

Rise Higher than your Resistance

After high school, TQ attended Mary Baldwin University, a private all-girls school in Staunton, Virginia. Certainly, TQ wanted to continue her love of acting and theater, so fortunately for her, Mary Baldwin had a theater program. To her disappointment, they often turned TQ down when she auditioned for significant roles. It became painfully evident that African-American students like herself were frequently cast in supporting roles as maids or servants. From the outside looking in, it seemed apparent that my sister's acting abilities were stronger than those awarded the leading roles. TQ became frustrated and felt the auditioning process was biased and unfair. One day, TQ and our parents sat down with Ms. Scott, a Mary Baldwin professor, to explain the adversities she faced. Ms. Scott posed a unique solution—TQ could write and cast plays to give African-American students more opportunities to perform. This was excellent advice, but it wouldn't be an easy endeavor, and it meant she would create something from the ground up.

With her professor's support and guidance, TQ created the foundation for The Kuumba Players. Kuumba means creativity in Swahili. She began to direct and act in plays she had written. The plays and characters were inspired by family members, particularly our grandmother, childhood events, or things she may have seen on TV or in other plays. The team began rehearsing in any space they could find available, as the main theater stage was not accessible to them. As an underclassman, TQ became quite an influencer. Word began circulating on the campus about The Kuumba Players. People would talk about the talented cast and how well the plays were put together. The tides turned when one of the productions was allowed to debut on the actual theater department stage. It was a big night for TQ. My parents and I were present to witness my sister as the writer, director, and leading actress. The Kuumba Players had a stellar debut performance. The play was funny, exciting, engaging, and memorable. The theater department staff were so impressed they decided to fund and support the Kuumba Players within the program. They even created a space for them to perform in the auditorium regularly.

Each year since, more African American girls became involved in this groundbreaking program. After graduating from Mary Baldwin, TQ would visit once or twice a year to mentor, advise, and train the new Kuumba Players. Her leadership and perseverance have provided a permanent opportunity for women of color to display their talents and skills at Mary Baldwin University. TQ gave these women a voice—a bold gesture that continues to shape lives to this day.

Pause and Reflect

What have you dreamt about accomplishing in your lifetime? Identify obstacles that may be standing in the way. Take the time to develop a plan of action. Think of someone who can help you troubleshoot and bring your dreams closer to reality.

Leave a Fearless Imprint

TQ was an angel who walked this earth, reflecting the light of Christ and changing the lives of all she met. With this fearless faith, my sister worked hard to attain everything God had for her in this life. I am blessed and inspired by her love and desire to benefit the world around her. TQ's life, legacy, and all that she stood for will forever remain engraved in the footprints of time. She indeed lived every day as if it were her last.

She never let fear stop her from fulfilling her God-intended purpose—to love and be loved, and most importantly, walk in his limitless strength. TQ walked with confidence as a daughter of the King. Her spirit was evident, like a queen, in how she spoke with a royal presence. This comes from knowing whose you are—you are appointed to a royal priesthood. My greatest hope is that her story and life heal the world and inspire others to reach for more, try harder, and dig deeper. TQ showed us we could all yield this kind of influence—making a lasting impact of legacy in whatever unique way we are called to achieve. Life is about sharing that love, strength, and inspiration with others. But it starts with you.

Pause and Reflect

Do you know who you are in Christ? How can you kindle the confidence that comes with being a daughter of the King? If you had complete confidence, what would you do differently? List three steps to grow awareness of who you are in Christ.

Leading in Prayer

Heavenly Father, I ask you to strengthen me today and help me embrace my identity in you. Please liberate my self-confidence and bring me to a place of fullness where I am complete and self-aware. Release me from fear of failure and the judgment of others. Give me the boldness to seek wise counsel and support as I move forward in your call on my life. Help me live each day as if it is the last and to leave a legacy that enriches the future and honors You. Amen.

This chapter is written in memory of TQ and her legacy by sister Nia Williams. Nia is an early childhood specialist in Atlanta and a social media content creator.

"I have always desired whatever I work on to parallel a message of truth, goodness, and beauty—it may not always be obvious, but I hope that my stories get people thinking."

-Christina Storm

Virtual Production Executive,
Director of Virtual Production at Netflix

Former Manager of Digital Production at Rhythm & Hues Studios, which won the Oscar for Best Visual Effects on "Life of Pi"

CHAPTER 18

Live in Impossible Possibilities

Katy Nichole

In January 2022, worship leader and songwriter Katy Nichole Litwiller released her debut single, becoming an overnight social media sensation. Amid a global health crisis, She penned the words to *In Jesus' Name* (God of Possible) as a response in her prayer journal. In childhood, Katy suffered from severe pain. During a time of heavy darkness, she almost took her life, but God had other plans. The song catapulted to number one on Billboard's Hot Christian Songs chart, breaking a 19-year record for a female artist's debut song and received an American Music Award nomination. Soon after, her follow-up single, *God is in this Story* with Big Daddy Weave, reached number one on the Hot Christian Songs chart. What appears to be Katy's overnight success was not a surprise to God as she now uses her testimony to share hope with others.

Only one in 10,000 babies is born with congenital scoliosis. I am one of them. It's known to be incredibly progressive and only gets worse with time. At the age of five, they gave me an official diagnosis. Doctors told my parents I might not walk and do normal childhood activities. I don't remember feeling limited as a child. Even in chronic pain, I would run, do backflips, and do anything I set my mind to do. I realize now I could not have done those in my strength. I did it with the strength God gave me, and He was constantly holding me up.

At 14, my condition progressed and it compromised my heart and lung functions. My spine needed to be straightened with the help of metal rods and screws. I thought the surgery would go smoothly and everything would be okay. Even after recovering from surgery, I was in daily excruciating pain and didn't want to get out of bed. I had severe depression and anxiety. My teenage heart felt like my life was taken from me, and I would ask God, "Why?" In one particularly dark moment, I was in a bad headspace. I looked at a bottle of pills sitting on my dresser and went to pick it up. All I wanted was an end to the pain, and I didn't see one. Immediately, I felt something saying I was not done yet, and my story wasn't over. From that day forward, I believed God had more in store for my life. For three years, with continual pain and difficulty, I trusted God's plan, which was beyond what I could see. Eventually, the medical team said nothing more could be done. The plan was to remove the rods and screws to alleviate the pain. Hearing those words brought me hope.

Later that same day, I saw one of the biggest rainbows ever. It was as if God was telling me everything would be okay and he was about to do something huge. I carry a rainbow keychain daily to remind me of his promise.

When I woke from surgery in the ICU, I had an encounter with the Lord like never before. I saw light shining into my room, but there wasn't a window. In those waking moments, I knew God would use my life, even though I didn't know immediately what it would look like. Miraculously, my spine was straighter without the metal rods and screws. Medically, that's not possible. I am grateful for walking through those three hard years. I look back and know not a single second was wasted.

Pause and Reflect

Have you experienced a physical, mental, or emotional illness that took you to a dark place? How did you overcome it? What lessons can you take from that struggle to bring glory to God's name?

The Song of My Life

In 2020, I started writing in a prayer journal. I've journaled my whole life, but I was very intentional about this journal. When everything shut down because of the pandemic, it was scary. None of us knew what was around the next corner. I wrote to help work through my anxiety. It was my way of handing it to God. Over the next few years, I started seeing God answer the prayers from that journal.

In August 2021, I was preparing to meet with fellow musicians for a co-writing session and had a panic attack. I felt God leading me to sit down at a piano. There, I wrote down the original words of the song, "In Jesus' Name." Let there be healing, Let circumstances change.

Over the next few months, co-writers continued to help me shape the song. It took time to capture the message I knew God wanted the song to have. The little viral clip I posted on TikTok with I pray for your circumstances to change, is the bridge of "God of the Possible." Throughout this experience, I knew the Lord was with me every time I wrote another verse.

Looking back, I see my life experiences led to this song. Because I've experienced ongoing pain and know his faithfulness, I don't have to be convinced that God is good. I see God showing up even in the smallest moments, and I'm continually in awe.

The song meant so much to so many people so quickly. I remind myself that it hasn't been about me because it isn't. I am privileged to be a part of this gigantic gift. It's incredibly important to have a group of grounded people around you. I have friends and strong relationships that have been a big part of this season. I praise God for every single little thing and I thank him for the opportunities I've been given. His provision for me has been a blessing because there were times when I could barely support myself. He has always provided exactly what is needed.

Pause and Reflect

In what ways have you handled anxiety and struggles in the past? What new strategies could you implement to include God in managing those difficult moments? How can gratitude change your perception in any circumstance?

True Confessions

I'm a little bit stubborn. Honestly, I have been strong-willed my entire life. It's been both my greatest strength and greatest weakness. I felt like I could do anything, and sometimes that hurt. Coupled with my faith in God, knowing there was no limit to who he is and what he can do, my stubbornness became a strength. It's helped my energy to keep going even when things are hard. A strong will can become a blessing if we allow God to use it.

In stubbornness, we must learn to be teachable. God has provided people to help me in this process. When people share constructive criticism, it's easy to feel defensive or defeated. I've learned to receive, evaluate, and apply when needed. Every person's unique perspective has potential value. If insights are immediately dismissed because of ego, we can miss out on an opportunity to grow. It takes a willing heart to be teachable and wisdom from the Lord to discern what others offer us. When I know someone has my best interest at heart, I want to be open and hear what they say. I can do this because we have a trusting relationship. There's never a time we can't learn and grow.

Pause and Reflect

How do you see God using perceived weakness to build strength in your life? Are you open to teachable moments? Who are the trusted and qualified people in your circle that can give you honest feedback? How can you be the same support to others?

Shining the Light

John 1: 4-5 says, "The Word gave life to everything that was created, and his life brought light to everyone. The light shines in the darkness, and the darkness can never extinguish it" (NLT).

In this world, it can sometimes feel like a dark cloud is hovering over us. Despite that feeling, God's love is always present. Even in darkness, I want to remind you his light is constant. When we understand this concept, it enables us to be his light to others.

Leading in Prayer

Heavenly Father, thank you for my life—all the mountains and valleys, and for my struggles and fears. Thank you for redeeming those difficult times by bringing your light and hope into my dark spaces. I ask you to continue to help me grow, trust, and walk boldly into the future you have for me. Help me listen to godly counsel, stay humble, and always remember that it's all for you. Amen.

"If Jesus gives us a task or assigns us to a difficult season, every ounce of our experience is meant for our instruction and completion if only we'll let Him finish the work. I fear, however, that we are so attention-deficit that we settle for bearable when beauty is just around the corner."

-Beth Moore

Evangelist

CHAPTER 19

Let Your Past be His Platform

Maureen Charles

Maureen Charles is a United States Air Force veteran, mother, grandmother, and lifelong Canton, Ohio, native. She is a woman whose neat handwriting fills the margins of her Bible. But she is not a convicted felon—not anymore. In 2019, Governor Mike DeWine launched the Expedited Pardon Project, designed to shave years off the normal pardon process. The bar to qualify is high, including at least ten years free of prison, parole, and probation. Only about three dozen people have received the pardons so far. Maureen Charles is one of them.

The moment I received that call will forever live as a freeze-frame memory. "Maureen Charles, I am the secretary for Governor Mike DeWine, and I'm calling today to let you know the Governor has agreed to grant you a pardon." At first, I was stunned. But as this impossible message washed over me and soaked into my soul, all I could do was squeal.

Joy filled my heart as I screamed, "Hallelujah! Thank you, Jesus!" into the phone. The Governor's secretary giggled on the other end of the phone as she began to explain the implications of this news—absolute exoneration from all my crimes.

The Early Years

My story didn't start there, of course. My parents divorced shortly after I was born. My father's alcoholism and womanizing were more than my mother could handle, so she left us in the care of our grandmother, Lucinda, a godly woman. She was broken-hearted over what my three older siblings and I were exposed to in our home, so she begged my father many times to let her take us to live with our aunt and uncle. But he always refused. Finally, after many months, he reluctantly agreed to let Grandmother take only me because I was the baby and, presumably, the most difficult to manage.

Aunt Frances and Uncle Money couldn't have children, so adopting me was their dream come true. They doted on me and sacrificed to provide for my every need. My uncle, who only had a second-grade education, worked in construction, and my aunt labored as a domestic worker for Jewish families. They fared well, considering their lack of formal education, but they wanted better opportunities for me.

My adoptive parents raised me in a strict but loving environment. They taught me to be honest, respectful, and responsible. They expected me to do my best in school and rewarded my efforts. But despite being nurtured and protected throughout my childhood, whenever I thought about my biological mother, negative thoughts and unanswerable questions assaulted my mind.

Why didn't my mother want me? Why was I the only one of her children to be taken away? Why was I raised as an only child?

I know now Satan was taking advantage of my situation and manipulating me into thinking I was unloved and not valued even though I had been told, and shown, countless times and in many ways that I was cherished. In fact, I received more love and care than my siblings.

But that spirit of rejection plagued my thoughts and hovered over me like a black cloud. When I became a teenager, I slowly began to act on those lies. I desperately wanted to feel accepted and to fit in, which led to me making poor decisions. I didn't even enjoy drinking or using drugs, but I had no self-confidence and got caught up in the act of being what I thought others expected me to be, not being true to myself and the values with which I had been raised.

Pause and Reflect

Write down any lies you have held onto from your growing-up or adult years that still cause you to struggle. How do those impact your view of how God can use you to fulfill his purpose? On the other side of your list, write down scripture that counters those ideas you have been tricked into believing. Ask God to overwrite those lies with his truth in your heart and mind.

Crime and Consequences

I got pregnant when I was 17 and gave birth to my first child. Then at 20, I had my second child. I knew I had lost focus and was heading down a dangerous path, so I tried to salvage what I could of the dreams in my heart by joining the U.S. Air Force. The military was good for me. I finally felt like I had a purpose—a new lease on life—and my aunt and uncle were proud of me. But sadly, my military experience was short-lived.

I set myself up by hanging around the wrong people and gravitating toward the same behaviors that made me want to join the military in the first place. When I got home, my situation only deteriorated. My friends and associates lived aimless lives spent manipulating others with no thought of improving their situations or the consequences of their illegal and immoral choices. It didn't help that we were all poor, living in the 'hood, with very few positive role models.

I got more deeply involved with alcohol and drugs, starting with marijuana, speed, and acid. I chose to give in to the highs I experienced and live in the moment rather than thinking seriously about living a productive life. I feared less and less, and curiosity became a motivating factor in exploring new and more dangerous outlets for my anguish and despair.

That's when I was introduced to crack cocaine, resulting in a rapid decline in my morality and sanity. I lived at risk daily and was getting arrested repeatedly for the same crimes: possession of drugs and paraphernalia, prostitution, robbery, criminal trespassing, and even assaulting a police officer. Even when I was out of jail, there were always active warrants for my arrest because I refused to appear in court at the appointed times and didn't pay my fines.

After many opportunities to turn my life around, it finally came to the point where the court ordered me to serve four months in prison. I had already spent most of my mandated sentence in county jail, but those four months in prison felt like a year, and a nightmarish year at that.

Abuse of inmates, limited medical services, and lack of mental health treatment were serious issues. Inmates had no voice and no hope. Old women who should have been home enjoying their grandchildren would die in prison before their sentence was complete. Pregnant women had a high likelihood of miscarrying, and those with potentially serious medical issues suffered unnecessarily.

Once, a fellow inmate fell in the dayroom during an epileptic seizure. She struggled for air and flipped around on the floor like a fish out of water. Several of us shouted desperately for help and sobbed while we watched helplessly. Yet we were all told to get back while the so-called nurse watched her suffer and threatened anyone who dared to touch her during the lockdown. No one in authority ever showed up. That was my breaking point. I realized then that if I didn't stop the madness of addiction and chaos, my life would end up in total ruin.

Pause and Reflect

Recall a breaking point moment in your life in which you had a hard choice to make that shaped the course of your future. What got you through that time? What were some lessons you learned about life and God's faithfulness and love for you during that time?

A Hard Turn to the Right Direction

When I finally got home from prison, I thought I had left all the misery behind. Child and Family Protective Services (CPS) assigned a caseworker named Terrell to me. He seemed genuinely kind, but it was clear his obligation was to look out for the best interests of my three children: Tina, age20; Lawrence, 18; and Jordan, who was just three years old. He explained I needed to start looking for a job as soon as possible and my children needed me. Uncle Money had passed away two years before, and Aunt Frances was now elderly and in poor health. Terrell told me he had talked with my aunt and children before I came home to determine their specific needs and challenges and that it was time to get my life together for their sake.

I smiled and said I would do whatever it took to keep my family together. I meant it. But when I started working toward building a new life, it became clear that my confidence was delusional. I thought being away for so long and determined to do better would be enough. But the monster inside of me was only asleep. I hadn't really dealt with the core issues related to my addiction.

Tina had started her second year of college, and Lawrence, my oldest son, was about to start his first year of college. Before they left, they, in a sad role reversal, said, "Mom, we're leaving home to make something of our lives, but we won't be able to care for Jordan. He's still little, so you'll have to do better." I assured them they didn't need to worry, that everything would be fine. But secretly, I was scared to death. After my older kids left for college, life went well for a short time, but with no support, it didn't take long for our situation to deteriorate. By then, they admitted my aunt into the hospital with pneumonia, and I felt like my whole world was falling apart. I didn't want to fail, but the odds were against me. I couldn't find a job, which meant I had no income. But the bills kept coming.

It wasn't long before they turned off the utilities. I kept Jordan covered with comforters as the weather turned colder, but the food was scarce, too. I had no family ties and was estranged from Jordan's father. My pleas for emergency help through social services agencies went unheeded. During this time, Aunt Frances, the glue that had held everything together and my only source of love and support, passed away. My heart was broken, but I had no one to share my sorrow. It was all too much. I started using again just to get through the sad, scary days, and it didn't take long for the neighbors to grow concerned.

I knew the day was coming, so when Terrell knocked on the door, then proceeded to remove Jordan from our home, I was numb.

I wanted to pray for help and healing, but I felt God wouldn't even hear me because of my lifestyle, let alone forgive me. I felt like I couldn't go on one more day.

Pause and Reflect

Are there chapters in your story that you think are beyond redemption, even by God? Have you ever felt your choices have thwarted any good purposes God might have for your life?

True Freedom

On November 4, 2021, at 10:30 am, I sat before the Ohio State Parole Board, joined by the director of the pardon program and two of my dearest friends. "Good morning, Ms. Charles. How are you today?" I responded I was grateful for this opportunity but also anxious. Then the meeting began. Twelve Ohio State Parole Board members started peppering me with questions about my past crimes, cases, and my life after incarceration. They covered my entire history thoroughly and systematically, as they were the ones to determine whether my case was worthy of the governor's consideration.

I answered each question, pausing as the reality of my terrible choices filled my mind. One member asked me what had motivated me to commit these crimes. I answered it was the drugs, but the response seemed too simplistic. It was my self-hatred and the belief that God had abandoned me just like my biological mother. I explained that I once had great aspirations. I had gifts and talents like all humans made in God's image. Before the drugs, I dreamed of being a great artist someday. I'd always longed to make a positive difference in the world. But I allowed drugs to overpower my life and became a different person than the woman of my hopes and dreams.

After some time, the interview shifted to the time since drugs and desperation controlled my thoughts and actions and how I had chosen to live my life after addiction. Again, I paused to reflect on the 30 years since my last conviction. I began by sharing some of the community work I'd done—helping to build Habitat for Humanity homes in Ghana, West Africa, and serving people in extreme poverty through countless mission trips to Jamaica. My team and I fed them, visited orphanages, built churches, and told these precious people the good news about Jesus seeing them and loving them. I also started Community Litehouse Ministries in my hometown of Canton, Ohio, a ministry whose mission is to help single mothers, children, and families improve their quality of life. The Children of Promise program was birthed out of that initiative—a grassroots youth ministry and safe haven for latchkey children ages 5-15. One element of this nonprofit was an after-school program that taught biblical principles to help shape character and build positive behavior in inner-city kids.

I didn't want to take credit for anything God had accomplished through me since my life of crime. I sincerely wanted the Ohio State Parole Board to know the deeds I had done were for the glory of God and out of gratitude for all he had done in and through me. "Ms. Charles," said the interviewer, "I understand you want to be modest. But do you realize you've changed an entire generation?"

I sat there stunned after that statement. I had never thought of it that way. I simply wanted to walk out the purpose God had shown me. As often as I had hoped against hope that someday I might be officially pardoned, I knew God would continue to use me to serve the hurting and helpless regardless of any legal proceeding or official title. I just had to be willing and trust him with the rest.

Perseverance, according to Webster's dictionary, is persistence in doing something despite the difficulty, or delay, in achieving success. The Bible teaches us to persevere in faith, trusting God to fulfill his promises. I am living proof we can trust that God sees and empathizes with our distress and God is faithful even when we are not. We are never too far gone for God to find us and redeem us through his kindness and love.

Leading in Prayer

Heavenly Father, you see me, and you love me. You have a great plan for my life, and no purpose of yours can be thwarted—no matter what. You alone can bestow a crown of beauty instead of ashes, the oil of joy instead of mourning, and a garment of praise instead of a spirit of despair. Help me turn to you, accept your forgiveness, and trust you with my story. Amen.

"The Kendrick Brothers auditioned many actresses from Hollywood for "The War Room," but God kept telling them, "No" because He had this role for me. It was an answer to the prayer I'd prayed 12 years before."

-Karen Abercrombie

Actress who played Miss Clara
"The War Room"

A Letter to the Sisters who have been "Torn Down in Purpose"

Precious Sister

I know you are blindsided. You were focusing on walking in God's call when life fell apart around you. Now you feel broken, bruised, and torn down by those you trusted the most. Your reputation has been dragged through the mud, but God has not revoked his anointing on your life.

It is painful and seems unfair, but know your Father, who still calls you, declares these truths over you:

> You have hope and a future. Jeremiah 29:11
>
> You will have trouble in this life. John 16:33
>
> He will never leave or forsake you. Deuteronomy 31:6
>
> You will reap a harvest if you do not give up. Galatians 6:9
>
> Christ overcame the world so that you may overcome this, too. John 16:33

It's time to get back up. It may seem the church has written you off and others have abandoned you—but God hasn't. No circumstance is too big to steal away your God-given purpose. Speak God's truth with confidence in the One who equips you. He desires for you to be reignited in your calling—out of the tomb like Lazarus.

Stand up and fight for his faithfulness even when you don't feel like it.

After heartache following a divorce and reconciliation that never came, He is birthing a fresh vision in me. Just as I am unforsaken—this is his word to you. His glory rebuilds his temple.

You can be assured, he is not finished with you. So come into agreement with his plan again, knowing He is faithful. Your Father is calling you forward, sister. Come out of the stronghold and walk confidently, knowing he designed you with purpose. You have a rich legacy and inheritance as a daughter of the King.

Fight sister. Be strong and courageous. Grow your influence today so you can build a lasting legacy for tomorrow. He is ready to rebuild you stronger, and the world is waiting for who God created you to be. Now go get her.

Andrea "Andi" J. Tomassi **is an award-winning co-author of the *Live Bold* devotional and host of the *Unforsaken* podcast. Andi travels and shares the message that no hurt is ever wasted. She encourages women to rise above their circumstances with integrity and grace. Her favorite place to write is lakeside and says you can never have enough pens, journals, or boots. She has three adult children and seven grandchildren who call her Mimi.**

CHAPTER 20

Desire to Go Deeper

Linda Goldfarb

Linda Goldfarb's vocal prowess has pleased domestic and international audiences for more than two and a half decades as a speaker, radio personality, performer, audiobook narrator, podcaster, and board-certified Christian Life coach. Her award-winning LINKED® *Quick Guide to Personalities* series speaks volumes to the readers, benefiting them in all aspects of relationships. Whether sipping frothed coffee with friends, hiking with Sam, engaging in deep conversation with her children and grandchildren, or speaking truth with gentle boldness, Linda strives to be transparent and authentic.

One crisp winter night in January of 1994, at the age of 38, I was warming myself by the fire. But I still felt emotionally and spiritually cold and numb. For as long as I remember, I was not fond of anything about myself. Growing up, I had a skin disorder and buck teeth. I was leery of letting anyone get close and most of my friendships sided on the shallow end of the pool. There were a lot of things about Linda that Linda did not consider lovely. I had an awful self-image. And I had gotten to the point where I just wanted to be okay with being me.

Dropping to my knees, I cried out to God through tear-filled eyes. Abba Daddy, please create in me a hunger for you, more significant than my love for my husband. Give me a thirst for you, for your Word, more remarkable than my love for my children. God, something is missing. I believe in you. I believe in Jesus, yet I feel empty. I need the filling of your Holy Spirit. Change me.

I went to bed that night, hoping my life would change, and God did not disappoint. When I woke the following day, I felt a strong pull back to the sunroom and an irresistible urge to devour God's Word. Mind you, I had been reading Scripture for decades. I was a good Christian girl raised in the church by godly parents. I knew all the Bible answers in my head. But that day, something felt different. God filled me with his Spirit in the wee hours of Monday, January 10, 1994. My head knowledge became heart knowledge, and God flipped my spiritual life upside down. He made me brand new.

For the first time, maybe ever, I felt free. Absolute freedom. God showed me so clearly that he was good with me just the way I was, which changed everything. A passion for relational transparency sparked in me, and by showing me how he sees me and allowing me to see myself through his eyes of love, the Lord released me from the shallow relationships I grew to expect. He opened my eyes and heart wide to accept others just the way they were. That close encounter with the Father filled me with new confidence, not based on myself, my appearance, or my abilities, but grounded in his love for me and his ability to use me in his plan. And while I couldn't fully appreciate it at the time, I now realize that was also the beginning of living out my purpose more fully. I wanted to tell everybody, "What God did for me, he can do for you." I've learned when the Lord gives you something to say, he makes a way to use every ounce of the gifting he has given you.

Pause and Reflect

Do you recall when God the Father, Son, and Holy Spirit became your all-in-all? Consider creating a timeline of your life. Start where you're most comfortable, and list the God moments you can remember. Observe how God has used every second to get you where you are today. No tear wasted.

Not Just Talkin' the Talk

In ways only God could have orchestrated, my radio broadcasting career launched in November 2009. Even though it was all new and we had so much to learn, my husband, Sam, and I agreed if we were going into radio, we would not pay for the broadcast. We felt confident that God would supply the funding. So, we prayed and trusted, then stood back and watched, amazed, as he brought huge sponsors for a radio show with no track record. *Not Just Talkin' the Talk* started as a local broadcast, grew to a regionally syndicated platform, and then went global via the internet. Simultaneously, my speaking career took off. I began writing, and after ten years of broadcasting, we retired from the radio show. God continued to open doors no man could shut with new opportunities to use my voice for his glory. I currently narrate audiobooks and host two podcasts—*Your Best Writing Life*, in association with the Blue Ridge Mountains Christian Writers Conference, and *Staying Real About Faith and Family*, my passion podcast. Leaning into my calling as a speaker and writer was exhilarating and fulfilling. But as daily obligations burned up my time and energy, I felt a nudge to slow down and reset. Yet, I wasn't willing to step back.

Out of the Gate–Spiritual Reset

I attended my first spiritual retreat in Oceanside, California, as a faculty member of a nationally known Christian speakers and writers organization. I was there for spiritual self-discovery, and on the second day, our group leaders informed us we were to remain silent for four hours to help us experience peace—not an easy task for a speaker and extrovert. We stayed at a working monastery, where the priests arose early every day, sang the Psalms, praised God, and worshiped as they performed their daily duties.

The first hour was agonizing. I thought, W*hat in the world is Bill expecting me to do?* I'm a type A, "get 'er done" personality, so I approached solitude like any other project—I worked at it. I wanted to follow the rules, but nothing about being quiet and still struck me as peaceful. I ran away from people so I wouldn't fall into my routine of speaking to everyone I met, thus breaking the strict rules of silence. Experiencing solitude felt more like a punishment than a gift. During the second hour, I made my way to the chapel. I reasoned no one would find me there and even if they did, they wouldn't talk to me. It seemed more natural not to speak in church, so I tried to settle in. When the third hour rolled around, I felt myself relax and went back outside. My breathing slowed as I walked freely around the monastery, marveling at God's creation. I saw people but didn't move away from them. A deep peace took the place of anxiety and dread.

During the fourth and final hour of my mandatory silence and solitude, I strolled back to my little cubby of a room. And there on the bed was a card. They instructed me not to talk, but no one said anything about reading. So, I opened the card. Inside was this beautiful note from a dear friend. The message read, "Linda, I'm looking at everything God seeks to do in and through your life. But sadly, you're like a Thoroughbred, wanting to break through the gate before God opens it for you. Consider sitting under your Master's training a bit longer because if you break through that gate too early, you may hurt yourself and others."

My friend's letter was jarring. But as I let what she said soak into my heart, I recognized the truth in those hard-to-hear words. As I meditated on the message, I realized I was so anxious to do good for God that I charged ahead without being in tune with him. And in that moment of acknowledging my spiritual thoroughbred-ness, I knew I needed training too.

A few weeks later, I attended the Christian Booksellers Association annual conference. I met and immediately connected with a fellow speaker, an amazing woman of God, with a powerful testimony. As we talked in my room after the event, I shared my thoroughbred struggle and told her about the note I'd received in Oceanside. She looked at me wide-eyed and said, "Linda, you don't know this, but I've studied the training process of Thoroughbreds. It's so fascinating and applicable to us, as believers, that I even talk on this subject." She explained the training starts when the horse is young and has a mind of its own and a fierce desire to do what they want to do. Since they are so strong in body and mind, they can be dangerous.

So, the trainer begins the process by taking the colt into the corral and leading it in circles for several hours at a time. All colts start by simply walking the same way repeatedly. In this way, the master helps the colt to focus on what is right in front of him. The horse cannot turn to see what or who is behind him. The training and conditioning occur every day, seven days a week, 365 days a year. This monotonous schedule helps the colt to be content under his master's leadership.

In the next step, the trainer leads the colt in a figure-eight pattern. The young horse passes the corral gate every time he completes a figure eight. Walking past the gate is when the temptation to buck the system feels strong again. Typically, his head turns because he wants to break out of that gate, away from the hand guiding him. But the master patiently leads the strong-willed beast over and over until he can eventually drop the lead and give the colt the ability to choose for itself. Those choices are surrender or rebellion for the colt—and us. As the master walks, the horse walks. When the master turns, the horse turns. He doesn't go near the gate or charge toward the corral. The colt is undoubtedly strong enough and can jump high enough to escape if it puts its mind to it. But he has come to trust the trainer and chooses to stop when he stops. When the master lifts a hand, the colt follows a specific command. Complete surrender. Then, and only then, does the Thoroughbred become useful for his purpose.

Pause and Reflect

Have you found yourself biting at the bit to charge into or out of your gate? What thoughts came to mind as you learned more about Thoroughbreds? How can you apply them in your leadership role?

God Opens Doors No Man Can Close

> **"These are the words of him who is holy and true, who holds the key of David. What he opens no one can shut, and what he shuts no one can open" (Revelation 3:7 NIV).**

I'm a strong, determined woman. Father designed me that way for his purpose, and I genuinely desire to follow his lead. It's not always easy, but surrendering to the Master's will helps me live out my purpose in peace, knowing he guides my every step. As we read in Revelation 3:7, God holds the key to all possibilities. Let us never take that lightly. Out of this challenging but beautiful process, I've learned three steps for living out our life's calling.

- ☐ Recognize our anointing
- ☐ Submit to our Master's training
- ☐ Release everything to the Lord's will

Recognize Our Anointing.

God has a purpose for us. He designed and gifted us perfectly to fulfill that purpose. If you're not familiar, or comfortable, with the term anointing, maybe my friend Brenda Blanchard's analogy will help. We can imagine that Jesus is the vine, we are one of the little branches, and a cluster of grapes is growing above us on the vine. As we walk out God's calling on our lives, it's as if those grapes are squeezed and poured out all over us. His goodness poured out on us for his glory.

Pause and Reflect

What would you gladly do without payment? Where have you seen God's success in your life? What advice do people ask of you? What do you get caught up in when you lose track of time?

Submit to Our Master's Training.

Just like beautiful, strong Thoroughbreds, we must be willing to walk in circles, to wait with patience and trust the leading of our Master. The enemy is always at work. He wants us to doubt God's timing and rush ahead in our own strength. But our good Father opens doors no man can close and closes doors no man can open. Trust him.

Pause and Reflect

Considering the last six months, do you feel spiritually rested or emotionally spent? Are you meeting deadlines or chasing them down? Do you want to go back in time to start again?

Are you leading others with a hard hand or a gentle nudge? In looking at your responses, what areas do you feel you need to surrender to the Father?

Release Everything to the Lord's Will

Four of the most challenging words to speak—and mean—are Thy will be done. We think we know what is best for us, our loved ones, and sometimes the rest of the world. But it's best to remember God is God, and we are not. He is love. He is good. He is trustworthy. So, release it all—your career, your spouse, your children, your health, your finances, your dreams, your doubts. Release all of it, to Abba's will, his way, and his timing. Allow yourself to feel these emotions. If you need to, close the door and cry. Shake your shoulders. Dance around the room. Receive. Feel. Release.

Pause and Reflect

What emotions do you feel upon releasing these areas to the Father? List ways you can proactively place your concerns for these aspects of life (career, family, health, finances, dreams, doubts, etc.) into the Father's hands.

My life, like yours, is an adventure, complete with potholes, pit stops, detours, and incredible destinations. Sometimes the pain smothers, but the beauty takes my breath away, too. If we wake up, we are going to struggle. My life will always be a work in progress on this side of heaven. God designed me on purpose, for a purpose. The same is true for you. And when we walk in his design for us, God's actions with and through our lives set us free to impact the world.

Leading in Prayer

Heavenly Father, I've made choices based on my limited vision. Without your guidance, I am bound to crash through many closed gates in my life. In the process, the thought of hurting others or myself knocks the wind out of me. Give me a hunger to know you more than ever before. Break my will to yours that I may become the thoroughbred, you designed me to be. Strong. Courageous. Humbled by your Spirit. Amen.

"Never be afraid
to trust an
unknown future
to a known God."

-Corrie Ten Boom

Missionary

CHAPTER 21

Let Grit Move You To Greater Things

Cherie Denna

Breaking free from a life of organized crime, outlaw biker culture, and sexual addiction, Cherie Denna experienced a radical rebranding of the soul. Her discovery of true belonging in Christ fuels her passion. She encourages and inspires the outcast, forgotten, and rejected to embrace peace as God's chosen and beloved. Cherie, a ministry leader, author, and writing coach, encourages women to utilize the hard things in life to fuel their faith. This kind of faith grows us as influencers as it allows God to use all of our experiences to grow something beautiful—reflecting his glory.

For as far back as I can remember, I lived by my survival instincts. Raised in a family of organized crime, including Sicilian Mafia and outlaw bikers, pure grit overflows in my DNA. I learned early on how to protect myself and those I love against neighborhood bullies. Running from that dangerous life at the age of seventeen took resolve, resilience, stubborn courage, and a boatload of brave perseverance. Faith did not come into the picture until a decade later.

When I asked Christ into my life, it took time to understand the journey and the healing that needed to happen. At the time, I was unaware God was going to use my experiences to grow me into the leader I am today.

This treacherous path helped me overcome hard things and persevere through challenges. I was able to adapt and bounce back when my world fell apart. My faith journey taught me to pursue God-inspired goals aggressively. I learned to hold firm to God's promises when I didn't hear his voice or see his hand in my life. Sometimes, perseverance is nothing more than the determination to show up.

James speaks of the joy and victory that comes after enduring adversity.

> **"Consider it a sheer gift, friends, when tests and challenges come at you from all sides. You know that under pressure, your faith-life is forced into the open and shows its true colors. So don't try to get out of anything prematurely. Let it do its work so you become mature and well-developed, not deficient in any way" (James 1:2-4 The Message).**

Pause and Reflect

What kind of tests and challenges have you experienced in life? During times of pressure, what aspects of your faith come to light? List some ways adversity has impacted you and your ability to lead.

Tenacity in Seasons of Transition

It took years of counseling, recovery, and support groups before I said Yes to God's calling to ministerial leadership. I wandered the wilderness as a recluse and even found myself homeless for a short while before he revealed his plan. The enemy worked relentlessly to destroy me in every way possible, but I clung to my faith with all the grit and determination I had within me.

As the Lord restored my life, He led me to Powerhouse Ministries. They were recruiting for a House Coordinator at their transitional living center for women and children. Intrigued, I picked up the phone and called them immediately.

Two months later, the posting was still up on their website, so I quickly submitted an online application while visiting the local library. On my way to my car, I listened to my phone messages. "Hi Cherie, I'm not sure if you are still interested in the job with Powerhouse Ministries, but I am finally returning your call from two months ago."

We can identify God's timing because it is simply undeniable.

Determination compels us to keep going as we seek the will of God. When life turns ugly, we get tired and fear the unknown, and sometimes want to give up. It is by God's grace that he carries us through. Within that first week, I began writing grants, which quickly led to leading Bible studies in the residential recovery program. These precious people, often perceived as outcasts, were my people.

Paul says in 1 Corinthians 15:10, "But because God was so gracious, so very generous, here I am. And I'm not about to let his grace go to waste. Haven't I worked hard trying to do more than any of the others? Even then, my work didn't amount to all that much. It was God giving me the work to do, God giving me the energy to do it" (The Message).

Pause and Reflect

What difficult or hard events have rerouted the path of your journey? List areas of growth or stagnation that occurred during those seasons? If you are currently in a place of losing ground, how can this experience be utilized to propel you into a new season of blessing?

Saying No to My God-Assignment

Have you ever said No to God? I did. In disbelief, I spouted, "How am I supposed to go back there alone? It is too dangerous, God." Why would God have me return to the dangerous side of town where I ran with the bikers years before? Here I was, five years after hiding underground, finally severing all contact with my past, and I am supposed to seek out my former partners in crime? I was comfortable in my role with the women at Powerhouse. It was a safe place for me. At times, when we rely on our emotions, our faith may weaken and open the door to the enemy's schemes to wreak havoc in our life.

It was as if I heard the Lord whisper to my heart, I invited you. Why wouldn't I invite them? Then, I remembered his promise to me from Jeremiah 29:11 to never cause me harm. Weeks later, I crossed paths with a brother who led a Christian motorcycle ministry. He acted on this directive, "Then the master told the servant, 'Go out into the highways and along the hedges, and compel them to come in, so that my house may be filled [with guests]" (Luke 14:23 AMP).

One by one, he began reconnecting me with the women from my past. Suddenly, we were planting a biker church in that old neighborhood. Each week, I stood before fifty or so bikers, testifying to all I had witnessed and sharing the gospel. This in and of itself was miraculous because in the male-dominated biker culture, women are considered property. We can trust the Lord to break through those barriers to accomplish the work he sends us to do. Opposition can rear its ugly head, but grit-fueled faith unleashes the miraculous power of the Holy Spirit to do the impossible. We can rest in the assurance that when God calls us to lead in the most difficult areas, the enemy does not have a chance, because God is our true source of strength.

> "Commit everything you do to the Lord. Trust him, and he will help you. He will make your innocence radiate like the dawn, and the justice of your cause will shine like the noonday sun" (Psalm 37:5-6 NLT).

Pause and Reflect

What is the scariest thing God has asked of you and why? How did you respond to his request? List three scriptures that can help you move forward in the face of fear.

Facing Injustice Head On

When I learned to forgive my childhood abuse and betrayal, I encountered God's true nature—to overcome evil with good. Along this journey, he connected me with people who were living, breathing agents of justice. With education, I learned to prevent, recognize, and react responsibly to child sexual abuse. Statistics enraged me while simultaneously igniting a passion to raise awareness within my church. I desired to bring proper training to our youth ministry leaders.

When I approached my pastor with the idea, he asked me to prepare a proposal, which I sent to him the next day. His response to my email went something like this, "While I recognize your strong leadership skills and passion for this cause, I believe you should pursue more healing before taking this on." What I perceived as a lack of concern only fueled mine. What about the children? Doesn't he care? If I'm not ready, why not get another trainer in here at the very least? I was not about to let anyone tell me God could not use me to bring about justice.

Soon after this disappointment, I attended my first Justice Conference, where thousands of Christ-followers shared a dream of impacting this generation. Led by World Relief, the conference attracted hundreds of ministries, churches, and nonprofits worldwide. I realized this was the perfect opportunity to use my grant writing skills for the kingdom. I began to help steward God's resources to bring justice to an unjust world.

The perceived rejection I experienced from my pastor allowed the Lord to redirect me.

It is crucial that we remain steadfast with our God-given assignment. Sometimes we misinterpret the direction he has for us. By God's grace, he led me into a much larger territory where my gift of writing intertwined with his calling. I founded The Justice Writer Group, a nonprofit providing pro-bono grant writing services. Our consuming passion, stewarded according to God's will, enables us to face injustice head on.

Pause and Reflect

When the world's justice system fails you, what is your response? Do you feel qualified to be an agent of change? Why or why not? What does God say about your qualifications? In what ways can you respond positively to what appears to be a closed door or a stifled opportunity?

Leading in Prayer

Heavenly Father, your love, mercy, and grace are more than I deserve. Your perfect measure of faith is my greatest gift. You know the desire of my heart is to walk in obedience to your precepts and the leading of your Spirit. Help me consider all my trials with a joyful heart, shifting my focus to you rather than my hardships. Temper my grit-fueled faith to stand strong in these times, forever in tune with the Holy Spirit. Amen.

"God called me to proclaim His Son and teach His Word. He did not promise that it would be easy. He did not promise that I would be safe, but He did promise that I would be secure."

–Robyn Dykstra

Author of *The Widow Wore Pink*
& Former Playboy Bunny

CHAPTER 22

Be the Light that Ignites Others

Jacquelyn Marushka

Jacquelyn Marushka, with over 30 years' experience in brand development and public relations, guides and coaches clients to advance their careers and dreams. Marushka Media (established 2016), the first Latina-owned PR and Branding agency in Nashville, Tennessee, specializes in music, film, television, and live events.

Jackie moved to Nashville in 1995 and became the youngest vice president of Public Relations and Communications in the Sony Music Entertainment system, responsible for 40+ recording artists across five record labels, publishing, film, and overseeing internal and external corporate communications.

In 2013, Jacquelyn launched the Nashville office for a Brooklyn-based PR firm (representing Bruce Springsteen, Lana Del Rey, Chance the Rapper, Elvis Costello, and more). In three years, the business outgrew her kitchen office to accommodate 15 clients

and 3 full-time staff. Led by a passion to help others, dedicated to living life rooted in gratitude and possibility, she runs a fitness program and serves the local at-risk community.

Growing up in the small farming community of Velarde, New Mexico, the star-filled skies taught me to dream big. The snake-filled mountains taught me to be present and alert. The flavor and color of our green chile and apple orchard harvest fed my love of light and story. My original hero, or shero, was my mom, Evelyn.

Every day, the alarm clock went off at 5 am. I could hear it through our thin trailer walls.

BUZZ. BUZZ. BUZZ. Like a loud goose honking as it flew overhead. But the noise never lasted long. Mom was up like lightning—no snooze button for her. Throughout my childhood, I never remember Mom going to bed or waking up. I sometimes wondered if she slept.

The shower knobs squeaked the water on and ran for several minutes. The water squeaked off and was followed by the "whirrrrrr" of Mom's purple mini-Conair hair dryer. Mom never allowed us to go outside with our hair wet—she said we'd catch a cold, so she led by example and made time to dry her shoulder-length, dark hair. Her soft dark waves parted down the middle, framing her face and highlighting her smiling brown eyes.

She turned the brass deadbolt on our heavy rough-lumber door that dad built from reclaimed wood and walked out to start her olive green 1974 Ford Fairlane station wagon with the wood paneling. Northern New Mexico gets cold in the wintertime. The skies are clear and bright blue, but the winter winds can cut through you like an ice saber.

Mom always warmed up the car, so it was toasty when we got inside. She woke my sister and me as the heater cozied up the green vinyl seats. As we got dressed, brushed our teeth, and combed our hair, Mom packed paper bags with snacks—not just for us, but for kids whose parents she knew couldn't make them lunch.

This is mom's nature. "Did you bring enough for everyone?" was part of her thought process. "Never let anyone feel left out. Be welcoming, be kind, always share what you have and don't worry if you'll have enough. God will provide for you," she'd say. Her teacher's desk had a drawer where she kept peanut butter crackers, peanuts, and cheese and cracker packs. When she shared snacks or full lunches, the food always came with wisdom and kind words of encouragement. Many of the kids she had in her classes didn't have love at home, and she did what she could to ensure each child knew they were important, capable, and worthy of investment. She made them feel seen by tutoring in math and reading or shooting baskets for basketball to help them feel included. One year, she volunteered to be our elementary school basketball coach. She doesn't do this for herself or to be mom of the year in anyone's eyes. She does this because kids matter to her. People matter to her. Now, more than 40 years later, having retired as superintendent of a school system, she still makes the most of every day and helps everyone from the youth she teaches at a small Christian school to her neighbors and, of course, her family.

Pause and Reflect

Is there a person in your life that mindfully helped you feel noticed, heard, and loved? If not, how could you have benefitted from someone who did so? How are you supporting others to feel seen and nurtured?

Going the Extra Mile

Mom has always gone the extra mile, working as many as three jobs at a time and working on our farm harvesting fruit to sell on the weekends. She always made sure we had enough to eat, clean clothes and always—and I mean always—did our homework.

Mom was an elementary school teacher who made ends meet by working as a cashier at a local dime store after school and on weekends. During summer breaks, when she wasn't attending summer school earning one of her three master's degrees, she was working on our small family farm picking fruit to sell at the farmer's market.

Some of my favorite memories were rooted in our time together, preparing for the weekend's summer farmer's market in Santa Fe. We'd first weigh our little green plastic baskets on a small, portable scale to get their empty weight. Then, we'd carefully place the apricots, cherries, and plums into the baskets, filling each basket to the weight of a pound. We'd sell each 1 lb basket for $3. Apples and pears (which we harvested later in the year) were placed into larger baskets but weighed in the same way, with the same scale.

What mom taught me, that her dad and mom (my Grandpa Mike and Grandma Sylvia) passed down to her, was that every detail matters and your integrity matters. My grandparents also imparted these four life lessons in words and example:

- If you take care of the little things, they'll take care of you.
- Always leave things better than you found them.
- Whenever possible, share your light with someone else.
- Overcome with kindness.

Those lessons were a theme through every aspect of their lives, and thankfully. I'm grateful to have had them as an example.

Every Penny Counts

My Grandfather used to keep a jar of change near his bedside. He'd empty his pockets and place that day's change in the jar. At the end of every month, I'd sit with Grandpa Mike at the kitchen table and help count every penny. We'd place the coins into paper tubes, which he'd take to the bank later that week. For helping Grandpa Mike do this, he'd pay me a percentage of those earnings. I used this money to start my very first savings account. By the time I was 15, I had $100 in the bank. Every penny mattered. If you take care of the little things, they'll take care of you.

Pause and Reflect

Make a list of ways you invest your resources such as time, giftings, and belongings. Is that investment producing growth in yourself and others—family, friends, colleagues, and acquaintances? Are there any ways that you feel God growing and expanding your stewardship vision?

Leave it Better Than You Find it

One day, I rode with Grandpa Mike to the grocery store in town. We went into Center Market—two coupon clippers with a plan and a purpose. Armed with his knowledge of the store layout, we worked our shopping list from the outside of the store inward. It was my job to look for the brands our coupons covered and to keep track of the fine print of how many items were allowed per coupon.

One day, as we walked into the store, Grandpa Mike noticed a few shopping carts scattered through the parking lot. He began collecting them and asked me to help. I asked, "Grandpa? Why are you picking up the carts when you didn't leave them there?"

He said, "MiJita, it's the right thing to do."

"But you didn't leave them there," I said.

"It doesn't matter. Let's just take them in. We're headed that way anyhow, right?"

"OK," I said, still unsure of why anyone would clean up a mess they didn't make.

On the way home, he explained that leaving things better than you found them is simply good practice. It's not about the person who left the mess, but if you see a mess, do your best to make it better. Taking those carts into the store was a simple way to make a small difference. And it was about us and our character. We weren't in any way being duped by someone too lazy to return their cart. It gave us the opportunity to show kindness and integrity.

That day I learned it isn't about anyone else but how I will react to those messes I encounter. I took this nugget into one of my first jobs in Nashville. Because I couldn't afford a gym membership, I applied to work at the YMCA of Maryland Farms, one of the fanciest YMCAs in the area. The only position they had open was for a custodian. It paid $9 an hour, but I got a free membership. It was a 20-hour-a-week job I scheduled on evenings and weekends because I still had my job at the film company from 9 to 5. I'd see music industry executives and artists daily, walking by as if I wasn't there. Occasionally, they'd ask me to take their dirty towels to the bin or ask me where the clean towels were. One day, I saw a man blow his nose into the gym towel and toss it on the floor by the weight machine he was using. He didn't think anyone would see him, but when he looked up, we locked eyes. I'm sure my expression told him I'd seen what he had done. I went over and picked that slimy thing up and took it to the laundry. I heard him chuckle as I walked away. Fast forward, five years later, when I was a newly appointed vice president of PR at a record company. One of my first meetings was with a manager and his struggling artist. They were going to come in for my help with a press campaign with which they had difficulty. Prepping for the meeting, I noted that the music was great and sales were growing, but I felt that the campaign was simply mismanaged. When the manager walked in, it all made sense in an instant. Why? The manager turned out to be old "snotty towel." This person lived life the same way in and out of the gym, cutting corners in his life, and in his clients' lives. I did what I could to help, but ultimately the artist parted ways with this manager, replacing him and his career took off.

The lesson is that a person's character, defined by integrity, spills over into every part of their life. If a person cheats or cuts corners in one area, it's highly likely they'll do the same in other areas. Colossians 3:23 says, "And whatever you do, do it heartily, as to the Lord and not to men" (NKJV). Whether it's picking up after yourself in a public setting or returning grocery carts, someone else was incapable of returning, always do what is courteous, not because of who may be watching, but because of your integrity. Always leave things better than you found them.

Pause and Reflect

How have you fostered the habit of leaving things better than you found them? What are small and large ways that you improve the atmosphere with your presence? Do you tend to be an absorber of the atmosphere around you?

Light Up the Room

My Grandma Sylvia's kitchen was the heartbeat of her home. She was up at 4:30 am daily to make coffee, tortillas, sausage, and eggs. Grandpa Mike was up at the same time, feeding his pigs and getting ready to go to the 15-acre orchard across the four-lane highway. When he returned, Grandma had breakfast ready. They'd pray for their food, sit together to eat, and then open their filling station and general store by flipping "on" the Texaco station light which sat atop a 20-foot-high signpost. It was a round, flat sign with a red Texaco star painted on it. There were two bulbs above the sign that lit up the star. That sign was the only one for miles and shined through the darkness, welcoming travelers to my tiny hometown.

There was something special about the light, the star, and its welcoming warmth. It represented safety, refreshment, and hospitality.

Grandma Sylvia once told mom that one candle doesn't dim by lighting another. If you use your candle to light someone else's, the first candle doesn't dim, but multiple candles brighten the darkness together. She also said your light burns brighter if there's more oxygen. So, the fresher air you let in, the brighter your flame.

Likewise, sharing wisdom, encouragement, your lunch, paper, pen, or smile—like a candle's flame—you brighten the world around you.

Matthew 5:15 says, "nor does anyone light a lamp and put it under a basket, but on a lampstand, and it gives light to all who are in the house" (AMP).

Outshine Life's Bullies

Now, this light doesn't just mean things. It can also mean stepping up for someone being mistreated, which takes bravery. I saw an example of this kind of light in the 7th grade. I was the new kid at a big school. I was much smaller than all the other girls and was picked on mercilessly by both boys and girls. It got to the point where I couldn't focus on my schoolwork because I feared many classmates. One September day, I was walking from my homeroom to science class. It seemed as if I walked 100 years down a narrow pathway past the gym to get there. This part of the day gave me anxiety because the walkway was lined with shade trees and had an overhang covering the concession booths.

The girls who used to bully me would hide in that shaded area. When I'd walk to science class, they'd call me names and say, "We're gonna get you." On this day, the group of six girls decided to pounce. I was most afraid of Colleen, as she was the biggest of the girls and the self-appointed group leader. Someone pushed me down from behind, and I fell forward onto my knees, dropping my books and cutting the heels of my hands on the asphalt walkway. I looked up to see Colleen walking toward me, saying, "You're gonna get it." I closed my eyes.

Then I heard a voice from behind me. "Get away from her, ***now***." I opened my eyes to see a dark-haired girl from homeroom with fists in front of her face—bouncing up and down on her toes like boxers do. All the girls scattered. She looked over at me. "Are you ok?" she asked.

I responded, "Yes. I'm just embarrassed."

She waited for them to walk away before saying, "I'm Michelle. Don't let them get to you. I have my class in the next room over. We can walk together to our classes if you want. This is Jennifer." She pointed to a slender girl with blonde braids, a gray and black plaid button-down shirt, highwater jeans, and a yellow backpack. "We walk together to avoid those bullies. It seems they only like to pick on you when you're alone. From now on, you will walk with us."

"Okay," I said. From that day on, we were the best of friends.

Pause and Reflect

Recall a time when someone has brought light into your life—shining hope into your darkness or igniting you to move forward. How have you responded in the past to the bullies of life? What actions can you take to incorporate being a light to others? Take a moment and list tangible goals to accomplish this task.

That school year reinforced what my mom and grandparents first shared, in words and by example—it matters what you do when no one is looking. God used my family to teach me the foundations of integrity, and that adversity can strengthen you if you let it. When we embrace these lessons, we grow in ways we couldn't foresee. The result often influences others to embrace growth as well.

"But he's already made it plain how to live, what to do, what God is looking for in men and women. It's quite simple: Do what is fair and just to your neighbor, be compassionate and loyal in your love. And don't take yourself too seriously—take God seriously" (Micah 6:8 The Message).

Leading in Prayer

Heavenly Father, thank you for loving me enough to challenge me to live with integrity. Let me reflect your light and love to those I encounter. Please open my eyes to opportunities where I can value, invest in, and inspire others. Help me hear clearly, and act without hesitation, when you speak. Lead me to be fair, compassionate, and operate in love. Amen.

"It's central for us as women to be providing mentorship. We need to be the voice that whispers and challenges. We all learn from each other. Women have unique skill sets when leading with vulnerability and nurturing. Vulnerability is a gift we can give each other."

-Leslie Ferrell

President/General Manager
Big Idea Entertainment

A Letter of Encouragement to the Daughters of the Father—The Most High God

Precious Sister

It's time you grasp the things Father has been trying to tell you. It's time you declared his truth over your life. It's time for you to wear the mantle you've been given and take your place in kingdom leadership on this earth.

God set you apart and appointed you. His desire is for his daughters to live without fear and doubt. As we unite with other women, we can help our fellow sisters who may have lost their way, in need of a helping hand or a word of encouragement.

Do not allow the circumstances or those who surround you to determine who you are. As you step out of your comfort zone, even when you're afraid, you are unstoppable.

You are more than a conqueror. You will be tried and tested when you stand in the face of adversity, the barrier of glass ceilings, and anything else life throws in your direction. In those moments, you will get back up.

Don't let the enemy divide our sisterhood with fear, apprehension, insecurities, or envy. We will build his kingdom together. We need each other. Remember, iron sharpens iron.

> "I have not stopped giving thanks for you, remembering you in my prayers. I keep asking that the God of our Lord Jesus Christ, the glorious Father, may give you the Spirit of wisdom and revelation so that you may know him better" (Ephesians 1:16-17 NIV).

He's here to help, and he created all women to win and all women to lead in whatever capacity they serve. He is saying, "Daughter, that includes you."

Dr. Vicki Harris desires to help as many people as possible as they grow professionally and spiritually in fulfilling their God-given purpose. She is the Chief People and Culture Officer as well as Diversity, Equity, and Inclusion for Our Daily Bread Ministries (www.odb.org). She has been married for 34 years and is a mother of three adult children.

CHAPTER 23

Tap into Your Resting Space

Veronica Clay

Award-winning spoken word artist and small business owner Veronica Clay has packed a lifetime of living and learning into her young adult life. At seventeen, this Kansas City native published her first book, *Mile Marker 17*, and hasn't stopped writing since. She is also a TEDx speaker, published poet, and public speaker. She started Veronica Clay LLC in 2021 to further build God's kingdom and empower others, awarding her first scholarship to a college student in 2022. Veronica hopes to give many more scholarships as God continues to open doors. She sees her strength in being a passionate learner and effecting change through dialogue. Her mission—utilizing her words to speak life, encouragement, and hope to everyone she encounters.

I like to say I've been attending church since I was in the womb. I was one of the kids who grownups came up to and said, "The anointing is heavy on you, child. You are going to do great things." What they said made enough sense to my kid heart for me to smile and shyly say thanks, but over the years, I began to feel the weight of their words. I felt like I was the protagonist in somebody's book, and the weight of others' actual or perceived expectations was heavy at times. I did my best to walk with wisdom, lead with conviction, and be the difference-maker Jesus and everybody around me was saying I would be.

As I grew older, I discovered my love for speaking and writing. I started speaking at churches, schools, weddings, and so on, as God provided opportunities. I've had the chance to share the gospel in all kinds of places, from bars and birthday parties to conferences and college graduations. I am so appreciative I was immersed in a God-fearing community that empowered a young woman to speak the words God gave her. I also recognized from an early age I was often carrying the weight of leadership in a way God didn't intend for me. I was pushing myself to speak at more and more events, even when I felt fatigued and sleep-deprived, because I thought that was what it meant to be a good steward of the gifts God gave me and a leader in my creative field.

This misconception became especially obvious in college. I often joke that everything was on fire during that time. I was overwhelmed, over-involved, and doing my best to be the best at every activity I participated in—which sounds ridiculous now. Still, logic isn't always the first reaction when you're experiencing all the pressure to meet deadlines and compete with fellow students. I was continuously pushing myself beyond my limits, trying to be a great spoken word artist, a great student, a great youth leader, a great public speaker, a great Christian creative, a great writer, whatever any of those things meant. I was experiencing burnout, and while college is exhausting for most students, a lot of my burnout was because I was trying to carry burdens Jesus never asked me to carry.

Now, I'm not suggesting burnout is always self-inflicted. Sometimes in life, there is simply a lot happening outside our control. However, how often have we taken on more responsibility or a chore we didn't need to at that moment? How often have we felt pressured, either internally or externally, to lead an event, take on a project, or serve at a church program we knew would leave us burnt out? Whether we choose to participate because we are afraid of missing something or feel we are not doing enough until we are absolutely drained, how many times have we said yes to a burden Jesus wasn't asking us to accept? How often have we felt God calling us to lead in a specific area and succumbed to the temptation to try to do it all at once?

Pause and Reflect

In what areas of your life do you feel overworked or burnt out? In what areas of your life are you holding your breath? Jot down a bullet list of these areas. Pause for a moment and recall each piece that causes you tension. Then, take a moment to breathe as you imagine handing each of those areas of your life over to Jesus. Now, ask God if there are any burdens you are carrying that he wants to help you remove from your life.

Resting in the Boat with Jesus

Imagine you are on a gondola, soaking up the sights and the sensation of floating smoothly through a city full of color and light. The gondolier points to historical landmarks, unique wildlife, and great restaurants as he gently guides you through the channel. Now, imagine shoving your hands in the water and paddling desperately, trying to get to the next stop. The boat isn't sinking. You aren't late. And even if either one of those were the case, you're not moving the gondola very effectively. After a few minutes, you're soaked, sweating, tired, and passersby are very confused as to why you got on the boat if you are so anxious and don't trust the gondolier to get you where you need to be.

It's a funny image until we realize we often do that exact thing. God has invited each of us to go on a lifelong adventure with him. We are excited to see the beautiful and fulfilling places he has promised to take us. We know his calling comes with work, and we are eager to please him. But the moment we become more fixated on the next project, task, spiritual work, or life milestone than on Jesus himself, we shove our hands in the water of everyday life and exert ourselves unnecessarily.

While I experienced burnout like no other in college, I now understand every phase of life can offer you the chance to feel overburdened. Whatever your calling, role, social status, or age, there will always be a list of tasks that need to be done. Whether you're a student, CEO, mother, volunteer, newlywed, caregiver, business owner, ministry leader, homeowner, fledgling author, retiree, or other role, there will always be an invitation to be overburdened.

I've allowed myself to slip into that hurried, overly competitive, overworked, and task-oriented mindset more than once over the last few years. It happens. And when I let it happen, I feel drained, discouraged, and disconcerted. I ask God, "How am I supposed to accomplish all the great things you've put on my heart when I feel so tired?" Nearly every time, he answers with one word,

Rest.

In our hurried culture that praises perceived success and glamorizes being overworked, Jesus asks us to fall asleep in the boat, go away to be alone, and slip away from the crowd. He calls us to rest.

Maybe that means setting aside one night a week where you stay home to rest. Maybe that means truly establishing a Sabbath day or two half days of Sabbath if your schedule won't allow an entire day. Maybe it looks like pausing and checking with your mind, heart, and body before you add another objective to your list. Maybe you stop and ask Jesus before you respond to the next invitation. I don't know what Jesus' rest looks like for you, but I know if we are constantly surrounded by people we need to serve, feed, lead, manage, or disciple, and if we are continually in environments that aren't conducive to rest, we simply won't rest.

No, I'm not suggesting everyone quit their job, toss out their family, and become a hermit. Even Jesus pressed into the community around him. He had compassion for the crowds, worked day and night to heal the sick and teach those hungry for the gospel of truth. He put up with religious leaders who hated him while also mentoring his disciples and building intimate relationships with Peter, James, and John. I'm not asking you to hide from people, places, or projects. I'm asking you—Jesus is asking you—to pause with him and have a meal, take a nap, and trust that the Great Commission he has called you to accomplish in your own unique way will happen, but not all at once.

Now, for those who feel resistant to this concept of rest, I've got a pretty good idea of what you're thinking because I've spent many years feeling that resistance, and I still do sometimes. Yes, we should be good stewards, do everything as unto the Lord, and look at the ants as inspiration for our work ethic. But don't get it twisted. God also rested on the seventh day and commanded us to do the same. What God is calling you to do is precious. Your work is valuable. And the Creator of the universe is asking you to set aside your load for a short time to be with him. Your heart, mind, body, and relationship to your Creator are also precious and have value. Yes, being a Christian means we must take up our cross and follow Christ, but we ought to be wary of picking up unnecessary burdens in addition to our cross and blaming God for the weight. He is calling us to rest.

> **"Then Jesus said, 'Come to me, all of you who are weary and carry heavy burdens, and I will give you rest. Take my yoke upon you. Let me teach you because I am humble and gentle at heart, and you will find rest for your souls. For my yoke is easy to bear, and the burden I give you is light'" (Matthew 11:28-30 NLT).**

As we pursue rest, we need to remember that even if we were to throw out our entire to-do list and all the people associated with it, there is a great chance our souls would still be weary because resting isn't solely about creating a space to be still but about drawing close to Jesus in that space. We can't find rest for our souls without involving Jesus in that restorative process.

Pause and Reflect

Do you feel weary and heavy-burdened, or does your soul feel well-rested? When was the last time you genuinely rested or had a moment to exhale peacefully and be fully present? How often do you have these restful moments a week? Do you feel you are resting enough or think God wants to offer you more rest? Take a moment to be still and ask God what he thinks.

Enjoying Creative Rest Continually

It is easy for me to say, "Get rid of your unnecessary burdens, and rest with Jesus." But what does resting with Jesus even look like?

I remember hearing an older lady at church talking about lying on her couch and resting in Jesus' presence, and the older women around her agreed. At the time, that sounded impossibly boring. I have a short attention span and am very squirmy. I struggle to sit still in public. You want me to sit still at home too? Not happening. Rest sounded too stifling and spiritual for me.

Thankfully, I learned the Creator is creative, so resting with him isn't a monolithic experience. There are a myriad of ways to rest with Jesus. If your spirit is drawing near to him and you are allowing him to remove your heavy loads and replace them with light ones, you are resting. Your rest doesn't have to look like others as long as you give Jesus a chance to restore you. Rest is not about completing a procedure but enjoying the experience of drawing near to the One who knows you best and allowing him to control the pace of your life.

Recently, I've pressed into exploring which styles of rest work best for me. I've learned to rest outside, enjoying God's creation. I've learned to rest in conversations with my family; instead of rushing to speak or say what is on my mind, I simply want to be with them. I've learned to rest while cooking meals by talking with Jesus instead of fixating on the finished product. I've learned to rest at work when I complete a task. Before diving into the next, I check in with Jesus. I tell him how I'm feeling and ask him about my pace. Often, he tells me to slow down, breathe, relax, and trust he will help me meet all my deadlines. I've learned I don't have to be obsessed with completing the next objective. I can rest in the completion of one task at a time. I can even rest in the middle of a task. I've learned to rest while driving, sometimes listening to worship music and other times being quiet with Jesus and admiring the wildflowers on the side of the road. I've found freedom in learning to rest. The more I incorporate, or embrace, opportunities to rest throughout my day, the more I feel at peace and fulfilled.

Pause and Reflect

Have you tried different forms of resting? If not, I encourage you to begin experimenting and asking yourself where, when, and how you most easily rest with Jesus. We rarely execute a vision without a plan. How do you plan on prioritizing rest if you feel you need more? Consider setting reminders on your phone, writing a note somewhere you'll see it often, or wearing a piece of jewelry that reminds you to rest.

Resting for the Sake of Others

If you are like me, caring for yourself may not be the most motivating or inspiring idea. Thoughts like, I'm fine, or This person needs me, so I'll keep going, even though I'm tired, may arise. You may have been motivated to read this book because you feel others need you to be a stronger leader. In Jesus's second greatest command, you probably understand and are enthusiastic about the "Love your neighbors" part. However, the "as yourself" clause is conflicting or completely lost because loving yourself is far less talked about in church. For some of us, loving ourselves is much harder than loving others. I get it. So, for the sake of the reader who struggles with prioritizing herself or feeling worthy of rest, knowingly or unknowingly, I will turn this conversation on its head for a moment.

If you do not see how resting is critical to your mission of loving others and fulfilling God's plan for your life, you need to understand this: When we do not accept the rest Jesus offers, we become less effective representatives of his nature.

It's plain and simple. When we are burned out, tired, sleep-deprived, skipping meals, and holding our breath, we are prone to be tense, angry, stressed, irritable, sick, short-tempered, impatient, hangry, discouraged, selfish, and so on. Even the holiest among us begin to look rather unholy when our physical, emotional, and spiritual needs are not met. This is not a flaw in our character; this is human design and reveals the need for our Creator. We are finite and designed to rest. When we don't rest, it shows in our feelings and behavior. Though we may be incredibly careful, our restlessness results in behaviors that will eventually corrode our best intentions and negatively impact the people around us.

I sometimes slip into the bad habit of skipping my lunch at work because I prioritize my workload over my well-being. At first, this all seemed virtuous because I finished my projects and met my deadlines. However, I'm hungry, hyper-focused, and irritable for the rest of my shift. I'm not paying much, if any, attention to my coworkers. I'm missing opportunities to connect with them or learn of areas in their life for which I could be praying. When I get off work, my shoulders, neck, and jaw are tight. I'm still hungry, and every car on the road is my enemy. By the time I get home, I'm either ranting about terrible drivers, isolating myself from my family, or being short-tempered because I have needs that weren't met in a timely fashion. Everyone and everything feels like an obstacle.

Could I go through an entire day like this without technically saying or doing anything sinful (that I know of)? Maybe. However, had I rested and cared for myself, I might have been more present with my coworkers and prayerful about their needs. I may have been more forgiving of fellow drivers and more attentive and kinder to my family. No, it's not a sin to skip lunch so I can work more. Sometimes it has to happen. However, when I allow myself to get into an unrestful routine, I increase my odds of not reflecting the heart of Jesus to the people around me.

The same goes for you, sis. Rest is a part of God's design for us, and when we try to omit it from our lifestyle, we begin malfunctioning. We slip in our words, snap at our loved ones, and miss out on opportunities to meet the needs of others.

Our urge to skip out on rest is kind of like the temptation to text and drive. Some people know they shouldn't text and drive, so they simply don't. Others are tempted to text and drive but value their life too much to risk a fatal crash. A few could not care less what happens to themselves, but do value the lives of others. Sadly, some drivers do not care about themselves or others, thinking they are skilled enough to take the risk. When people text and drive, they reduce their ability to be alert and lessen their response time. In the same way, when we forgo God's rest, we decrease our chances of effectively reflecting God's nature. If we truly desire to love others, we choose to rest, to offer them our best selves.

If you are not in the headspace to rest for yourself, rest for the sake of others. God wants you to understand his purpose in resting to expand your potential as an ambassador of love, hope, and peace.

Pause and Reflect

Are there areas in your life where your lack of rest may negatively impact others? Ask God to reveal these areas to you and write them down. Ask God how you can be more intentional about resting in these areas. Why do you rest? Do you rest for others, yourself, or because God commands it? Ask God to reveal his heart for you and reason for designing you with the need to rest.

Silencing the Buzz

Those who feel the pull to leadership often feel a deep sense of urgency to build whatever they are called to build as soon as possible. This urgency stems from excitement and pure zeal to please God, accomplishing the work he has called us to. Problems arise when we allow this buzzing energy to finish, accomplish, and build to become our focus.

God is so happy we are excited about what he has called us to, but he is even happier when we nestle in close to his heart and trust him to take us where he has promised at his pace. We have the rest of our lives; regardless of age, that is enough time for Jesus to do the extraordinary. He can do more in one minute than we can in a thousand lifetimes. Don't worry about the timeline. We can follow his slow, gentle pace, trusting he will fulfill his promises and accomplish his plans in his timing. We can rest in that truth. We can rest in him.

Pause and Reflect

What would it look like if we accepted God's promise to us, his visions and calling for us, with a heart that is at ease? What could it look like to restfully say, "I will follow?"

Leading in Prayer

Heavenly Father, my soul longs for rest. Make me lie down in green pastures. Teach me to embrace the rest you offer. Show me the burdens I am carrying that you aren't asking me to carry. Give me the grace, wisdom, and peace needed to remove those burdens. Help me follow Christ's example by making time and space to rest in you. Remind me to savor the countless ways I can enjoy your presence and exchange my heavy burdens for your light load. May I become a restful leader who points others to you. Amen.

"What if Christians were known as a countercultural community of the well-rested—people who embrace our limits with zest and even joy?"

-Tish Harrison Warren

Author in *Liturgy Of The Ordinary- Sacred Practices In Everyday Life*

CHAPTER 24

Nurture a Team that Can Survive Without You

Lisa McIntire

In 2003, Lisa McIntire received a devastating auto-immune diagnosis that radically changed her life. She was told it would be miraculous if she lived to see her 50th birthday. One year before that expiration date, she woke, acutely aware that this day represented a unique opportunity—to journal through the last year of her life. A few months after her 50th, she received another devastating diagnosis.

Lisa started as a Certified Public Accountant (CPA), bringing solutions to the business world. In 2016, Lisa transitioned to serving as the Executive Director of a non-profit—offering hope and building healthy families in her community. As a blogger at *The Last Birthday* (thelastbirthday.com), Lisa shares her journey. Her heart is focused on helping women live well, love well, and lead well—embracing every day to its fullest.

Life and leadership present us all with unforeseen challenges. In 2021, I found myself amid another health crisis—breast cancer. I found a large lump just eight weeks after receiving a clear mammogram report. That discovery turned into a full year of treatments and surgeries designed to be more aggressive than the insidious disease.

I have been leading people in formal roles for almost two decades, and my leadership philosophy and approach have morphed through the years. But one thing that hasn't changed is my belief that every person is hardwired for significance. God endows us with gifts and talents that he intends necessary for the work he puts before us.

The most rewarding part of leadership is helping people align their strengths and passions with a particular organizational role. I love watching their natural creativity shine as they embrace the role and contribute in ways only they can. Having been charged with turning two teams around, I have experienced firsthand that when all team members work from their strengths, the sum of the parts becomes much greater than the whole. The individual employees and hence the organization, flourish.

I see my role as active support, developing, and resourcing the team so they can be the best versions of themselves. I love being eyeball-to-eyeball with my colleagues—encouraging and empowering them in whatever ways they need. There's something about just being there, swept up in the hum of the day in the place where we all carry out our calling.

But that was all stripped away on D-day—diagnosis day June 3, 2021. Chemotherapy and Covid are a particularly deadly duo with compromised immunity, so my oncologist issued strict orders that I was to work from home immediately and throughout treatment. The prospect of five months of chemo and at least two surgeries meant my life and leadership were about to change drastically.

As Executive Director for a faith-based nonprofit, I serve several stakeholder groups: clients, employees, volunteers, Board members, business sponsors, church partners, and individual donors. It means I spend a lot of time in the community promoting our mission and message. But that all came to a screeching halt, too.

Suddenly, leading in all familiar ways was no longer feasible. Fear flooded over me, and I wondered how in the world I could lead in this situation with cancer, from home. It seemed impossible, and I fully expected my Board of Directors to concur.

But they didn't. They graciously assured me they had confidence in my ability to discern the Lord's leading and direct the organization through this crisis. They would do whatever they could to support me in the process. Their encouragement assuaged my fear of losing my job and health and gave me the presence of mind to start thinking creatively.

Having come through cancer and returning to the office as I write these words today, I've reflected on the past year hoping my experiences can help others, whether leading through illness or any other crisis.

Pause and Reflect

How are the teams and relationships you are involved with strengthened by your gifts? Recall a season in your life when you feared what was coming next. What surprised you about how people did or did not respond during that time? How did you cope with or without the support of those around you?

Build a Foundation of Trust

As cliché as it might sound, the key to our organization surviving and thriving during my cancer journey was, in a word—trust. If you had asked us before my illness if we trusted God and each other, we would have answered with a resounding, "Yes." We all agreed and frequently reminded each other that God is all we need. He is the CEO of our organization, and no frustration or difficulty is too complex for him to handle. He loves us and wants to help us help others.

It sounds so sweet and simple. But as my eyes scan back over those words, I want to laugh and cry simultaneously. Don't get me wrong, every word is true. God is trustworthy. He is good. He is above all and beyond all. But the trials my team and I have faced over the last couple of years have tested our faith and driven home Jesus's words in John 15:5. "Apart from me you can do nothing" (NIV).

I had to communicate my situation clearly and candidly to continue growing in trust as a team. Being open with our team or stakeholders about our personal problems may feel uncomfortable for many leaders. But without accurate information, the natural result is team members will fill in the knowledge gaps with the best information they have, which might not be factual. When that happens, a lot of time and energy get wasted unnecessarily.

If I could convey only one message, condensed down to two words, from this sad, scary year, it would be—Trust God. This lasting principle for life and leadership encompasses all situations—tragedies, triumphs, highs, and lows. Leading through Covid and cancer, plus all the normal pressures and priorities all leaders face, has convinced me more than ever how critical and how freeing it is to live by this foundational truth.

Pause and Reflect

As a leader, how difficult is it for you to relinquish control of any situation? List a significant moment requiring you to trust in God, not your strength. How has identifying the abilities those around you possess helped you relinquish control of the details?

God cares about you. Period.

God cares about you, but he also cares about your work and promises to provide whatever you need. We, or at least I, tend to think of provisions pertaining to finances or God stepping in when we have come to the end of our rope. But leading through my cancer diagnosis demonstrated God intends for His promises of provision to be all-encompassing.

If we're honest, we all need many things every day. But how often, when we are healthy or energetic, do we stop to give our anxieties to God and trust him with the outcomes? It's so natural for us to just dig deeper and hustle harder, trying to solve our problems and meet our own needs. That mindset only leads to frustration, burnout, and hitting the proverbial wall. But sometimes crashing headlong into a massive wall like, well, cancer, is the wake-up call we need to realize that we were never meant to live this way. When you're sick, weak, and tired, you become acutely aware of your lack of energy, faith, peace, money, relational connections, and much more. But God is our compassionate Father who wants to provide for all our needs.

Pause and Reflect

What are your go-to coping mechanisms when you feel all your options are exhausted? In what ways are you intentional about taking your needs and anxieties to God first?

All He Requires is that We Ask

One evening, a couple of weeks after my bilateral mastectomy, I rode with my husband to run an errand. Steve ran into the store, but I stayed in the car. I was feeling discouraged, overwhelmed, and exhausted. My mind was running wild with worry. Instead of focusing on how far I had come, I started thinking about everything unknown or undone—a body I didn't recognize, outstanding medical bills, loads of dirty laundry, and many unanswered questions. You get the point. Then, right in the middle of my meltdown, I felt one little word, gentle but firm, rise from deep within. Ask. Then the rest, Ask, and you will receive.

So, I did. Right there in that parking lot in the darkest season of my life, I spilled it all. Through hot tears, I told Jesus in explicit detail about everything filling my mind and tearing at my soul. At that moment, as I released the pent-up fear and came face-to-face with my vast emptiness, I knew I had a choice—I could worry, or I could trust. It's easy to think we trust God because we've trusted him with the big things like eternity. Most often, we are primarily operating from our strengths, implementing our ideas, and relying on our intelligence. During a particularly difficult leadership season before I got sick, I was trying, not trusting. No matter what I did, what bright ideas I had, and how hard I tried, situations just kept getting worse.

Trust is a hot topic in almost any leadership book. Two-way trust, between leaders and team members, is crucial to creating healthy organizational cultures. But other elements of trust are just as important. Not only do you need to trust God and your colleagues, but you also need to trust yourself, your intuition, your knowledge, and your experience. Trusting the process is important too. Trust that the values, vision, plans, and procedures you and your team put in place will stay solid during unsettled seasons.

Pause and Reflect

Can you give an example from your personal life that focuses on how differently ***trying*** and ***trusting*** affected the outcome during a time of crisis? Think of ways to build upon the strength of two-way trust with collaborative endeavors. Who do you have the hardest time establishing trust with—God, others, yourself? Why?

Surround Yourself with a Top-Notch Team

When you are limited physically, it also affects your ability to function mentally and emotionally, which are crucial to leading well. Even on the best days, leadership takes an enormous amount of energy. But tapping into the energy that used to flow freely feels like an impossible task when you're sick or stressed. It's like trying to draw up water from a dry well. You need an excellent team to carry out the mission with you.

A high-quality, self-motivated team is essential for any organization to be successful. If this doesn't describe your team, or if you have weak links, start working to rectify that now. The process of building and strengthening your team should start before a crisis. Trying to build or restructure your team when you are less physically or emotionally present will only add to your stress.

Let's discuss what it means to have a top-notch team. I've learned the hard way (which is how I've learned most of my life and leadership lessons) that hiring hard-working or exceptionally positive people isn't enough. Simply showing up for work on time and handling their duties competently won't get your team through difficult situations. You need men and women of impeccable character with hearts of humility, willing to focus on the organization's mission. For the organization to thrive in a leader's physical absence, each person must know their role, stay in their lane, and be willing to leave their comfort zones behind in this new frontier.

Pause and Reflect

Think about the support team or people you currently have around you. What would be the outcome if you were in crisis and had to relinquish your full duties today? What can be done to rectify any weakness proactively? In what ways can you not only be a great worker handling your business, but also be considered having impeccable character and humility with a willingness to focus on the mission?

Embrace Technology

Depending on your natural aptitude for and comfort level with all things techy, it's possible you, like me, have a love/hate relationship with technology. As overwhelming as learning new ways of doing things can be, using technology to build a bridge between you, your team, and stakeholders can be a game changer. Thanks to Covid, we all became more adept at working from home, for better or worse. Navigating the Covid crisis forced us to become more familiar with electronic ways of communicating and conducting business. We're all sick of phrases like, You're on mute, but during my health crisis, I was so thankful for those Zoom meetings, which served as a lifeline to the team I missed so much.

Other than times on Zoom, I spent many hours every week in the cancer center with sick people and people who took care of sick people. My world shrank significantly during that time, and technology was my only way to connect with my inner circle, personally and professionally. Except for Wednesdays, when I felt the worst, staff and board members would text with anything urgent, another quick form of communication. We sent everything else through email.

Email was also a lifesaver. Because of the timing of my chemotherapy treatments, I usually felt the best on the weekends when no one else was in the office. But because most of our communication during that time happened over email, I was able to tackle the more urgent matters throughout the week. I tackled the issues that require deep thinking or a more thorough response on the weekend when I felt better. The team knew they would receive a response to any outstanding items from the prior week in their inbox on Monday morning.

Pause and Reflect

What are some ways you've creatively had to rethink the use of technology, currently at your fingerprints? What keeps you from learning how to use technology or any resource more consistently and efficiently tapping into all it offers? How could a more defined time-management strategy (weighing what is urgent against those things that can wait) benefit team-focused productivity?

Practice Self-Nurturing and Healthy Boundaries.

We hear so much about the importance of self-care, but what images are conjured up in your mind when you hear that term? Soaking in a hot bath? A spa day? Healthy food? A beach vacation? While I suppose all those things can fall into the self-care category, times of crisis accentuate all the areas where we have not cared for ourselves well. The stress and grief of these times also make it difficult to focus and force ourselves to take the necessary steps to nurture our bodies and souls.

When life seems senseless, these moments of nurturing ourselves or allowing ourselves to be nurtured by others make it feel better. They help us believe we can make it through one more day, and connect us to deeper parts of ourselves that transcend our current circumstances. Provided you allow it to, a crisis clarifies priorities. Walking through a crisis has a way of peeling away the superficial layers to the core—the essential responsibilities and the tasks that flow from those duties. Then it's about spending your time and energy—your most limited resources, especially in a crisis—fulfilling those roles.

By its very nature, illness taxes your physical, mental, and emotional reserves. It's impossible to be all things and do all things. But it's easier to deceive ourselves into thinking we might just be the first human for whom it is possible when we are healthy and energetic. It's much more difficult to lie to ourselves when battling illness or walking any rough road. When you are low, spending your precious energy on frivolous activities will only bring you lower. Our culture has a common yet unfortunate misconception that busyness is synonymous with productivity—that activity automatically translates into fruitfulness.

So many of us are guilty of proudly wearing what I like to call the busy badge. We want everyone we meet to know how overwhelmingly busy we are. That's often the answer to the "How are you?" question, and we take pride in being so busy that we meet ourselves coming and going. Not only is being busy for the sake of busyness, not something to be proud of, it is also dangerous. It is dangerous to our health, relationships, and connection with God. He never told us to be busy. He told us to bear fruit. And trust me, it's not the same thing.

Bearing fruit in our lives isn't even possible if we are in perpetual motion. This topic could be an entire book unto itself. We are not designed to live in a constant state of sensory overload. But we don't seem to realize how much of the activity we busy ourselves with is truly optional. In our personal lives, we may think nothing of spending hours scrolling through social media pages, mindlessly shopping online, or ingesting an unhealthy amount of television. Even at work, we can fall into the trap of reading every email newsletter that finds its way to our inbox or saying yes to unnecessary meeting requests. It's a constant battle to say yes only to the essential things that we can do well, particularly when our health requires extra attention. Let others do what they do, and you play your role. That's how the whole of our organization ends up being greater than the sum of the parts.

Pause and Reflect

What are some items that fall through the cracks when you are pushed to your limits? How often do you exchange your health, relationships, and connection to God for busyness? Create a way to identify those things that keep you in a state of busyness, preventing you from connecting with those that matter.

Work Yourself Out of A Job

This might seem counterintuitive, but great leaders strive to work themselves out of a job versus striving to ensure they are always seen as the person in charge. They do this by prioritizing and developing others, which can be scary, especially when life already feels unpredictable or out of control. It can be tempting to fear the future and hold on tighter if you sense your team or organization no longer needs you actively mentoring. I know. I've been there. I'm there now in some ways.

Feel those feelings. Accept them as a natural, normal part of the leadership arc. Then move forward again, trusting God and your team. Know that acting with integrity and prioritizing others' best interests will never lead you astray.

During my illness, one insight God gave me early on was that I needed to make a choice—to surrender to God every single cell of my body and all the moments of my life or to take the reins myself and turn from him in bitterness.

Pause and Reflect

What are your thoughts about the concept of working yourself out of a job? How does your trust in God and your team impact this concept?

Decide You are Enough

I had to decide when all the externals—my health, appearance, social connections, and leadership role were all stripped away, I was still enough. Who was I if I wasn't the Boss Lady? Was I enough when the only thing I accomplished in a day was brushing my teeth or taking a bath? Was I worthy when I spent day after day lying on the couch because I was too dizzy or weak to read a book or watch television? Did I matter when I just slipped quietly out of life's landscape and into an abyss so deep and dark that the prospect of death seemed like a comfort, a welcome release?

The answer, I learned, for me—and you—is yes. We are enough when our bodies break down, when our worlds implode, and when we aren't productive. We are enough when we must use every ounce of energy to fight through another day, just surviving but far from thriving. We must decide being a child of God is truly enough. No matter what. Only then can we lead ourselves, our families, and our teams from a place of humble confidence, generosity, and wisdom. As we put one foot in front of the other, holding the Father's hand and following his lead, we will rise from the ashes and discover a new level of depth and beauty in our leadership journey.

Thanks to leading through illness, I know for sure that our God delights in birthing new dreams in our scarred hearts. Trust him. Trust your team. Trust yourself. Then lean into life and leadership. God will take care of the rest.

Leading in Prayer

Heavenly Father, thank you for this privilege of stewarding people's souls and leading others. Help me lead like Jesus—humble, wise, and connected to you. During a crisis, grant me wisdom and the ability to trust you through it all. You promise to work all things, even this, for good. May I remember you are in and over everything. You don't need me. You choose me. You promise never to leave or forsake me, which gives me the courage to move forward in leadership and life. Amen.

"I've never scored a goal in my life without getting a pass from someone else."

-Abby Wambach

Soccer Player

CHAPTER 25

You Be You

Babbie Mason

For Gospel Music Hall of Fame inductee **Babbie Mason**, living life in a performance mode, which started early in her childhood at her father's church, was the only life she knew. Babbie's roots trace back through five generations of pastors. Ministry is in her blood. The church stage was comfortable, familiar, yet an easy place for the real Babbie—the Babbie God knew—to slip into the shadow curtained by the expectations of others.

This award-winning singer, songwriter, author, talk show host, and adjunct professor of songwriting at Pointe University and Lee University finally made a remarkable discovery. God didn't want her to continue hiding her true self. Babbie wants you also to discover the beautiful leader he's created, who is authentically, unashamedly, 100 percent you.

Have you ever felt you were different? That you didn't fit in? I get it. I struggled to be at peace with who I am for many years, particularly related to my musical style. I have loved music from as far back as I can remember. It was easy for me to play the piano by ear as a kid. I could listen to a song, sit down at the piano, and play it without any sheet music. I have a fond memory of being in the first grade. We had an old upright piano in our classroom. When our teacher had to dash across the hall to the school's front office, she would leave me in charge of entertaining my classmates until she returned. This musical gift earned me a full-time job as the church pianist and choir director in the church where my father was pastor. They hired me at age nine, and I played for the church for almost 20 years. After graduating from college, I met my husband, Charles. Then I moved from Jackson, Michigan to Atlanta, Georgia.

During those years, I grew up singing the traditional black gospel music of the '60s and '70s. The songs of Mahalia Jackson, Roberta Martin, James Cleveland, the Consolers, the Caravans, and the Nightingales defined the music of my early childhood. We sang their music every Sunday in our Baptist church choir. As I approached my early 20s and searched for my way as a musician, my style became less traditional and more contemporary. My musical sound became more middle of the road. As a budding solo singer, I gravitated toward the style of both black and white singer/songwriters of that decade. Blaring from the speakers on my record player in my small, second-floor apartment, you'd hear the music of contemporary Christian and gospel singers of that day. I emulated the music of both black and white singers such as Andrae Crouch, Edwin and Walter Hawkins, Dannibelle

Hall, Evie Tornquist, Beverly Glenn, Second Chapter of Acts, and Honeytree. I was also greatly influenced by women who sang and played the piano. I easily belted out the songs of Aretha Franklin, Carole King, Nina Simone, Karen Carpenter and Roberta Flack.

In the early '90s, I entered the contemporary Christian music industry. I wrote and recorded songs like *All Rise, Each One Reach One, Standing in the Gap, With All My Heart, God Has Another Plan, Pray On,* and *In All of His Glory.*

Pause and Reflect

What leadership qualities do you admire in others? Which of these qualities do you see in yourself? How have you seen God use these qualities in you?

Being the Misfit

I've never had the kind of voice that resembled many black female gospel singers. People often would hear my music on the radio and assume that I was a white woman. Then they would attend my concerts and be surprised to find I was black. If I can be honest, that used to mess with my head. I felt I was a misfit or that I was weird. I convinced myself that my music sounded too black for white people and too white for black people. There were many days that I felt inadequate about my music and self-conscious about my voice. I felt as though I were gray.

Over time, though, I began to see something uniquely beautiful occurring in my concerts. From the stage, as I was singing in concert, I'd look out over the audience and see a gathering of the body of Christ represented consistently in those who attended my concerts. It is beautiful to see a blend of different races, denominations, and cultures coming together to worship the Lord.

Back in those days, quite frequently, I was the first black person ever to stand on the platform to sing in many southern white churches. Until they opened their doors to a Babbie Mason concert, a blended gathering of believers had never occurred in many churches. God has used and is still using this ministry as a bridge to bring people together in worship instead of a category that keeps people polarized. Being a bridge can be difficult—even painful. Bridges help people cross over to the other side. Bridges take people over treacherous waters. And bridges get stepped on because they connect people. All of that can be uncomfortable at times. But bridges also help us overcome obstacles. They inspire us and take us to places we could never reach without them. Bridges usher us to an apex—a vantage point that wouldn't be seen without them. For over three and a half decades, God has allowed me to usher people into the high places of his presence. In that regard, I'll be a bridge any day.

Pause and Reflect

In what areas of your life do you struggle with feeling like a misfit? Do these feelings impact how you view your leadership potential? Are there any aspects of your life where you can identify with being a bridge? How could you shift your thinking to utilize perceived weaknesses and find joy in using who you authentically are to help others?

Celebrating Uniquely Me

When I saw God was using my voice to bring people together, I celebrated the distinct quality of my voice and God's unique calling on my life. I stopped seeing myself as weird and started seeing myself as unique. I began to walk in my destiny and call with confidence. I have learned that most often, the very thing we think is the strangest about us is the same thing God wants to use to set us apart and establish our uniqueness for his glory.

God will use what we consider a weakness or liability to show himself strong.

In 2 Corinthians 12:9, the Apostle Paul reminds us of what our Lord told him during his struggle. “My grace is sufficient for you, for my power is made perfect in weakness” (NIV). I thank God for those who showed me the way and gave me great music to imitate. I praise God for their musical gifts. Those artists I mentioned and many more that I didn’t were excellent role models for me. But eventually, I had to find my way and be true to myself and God’s purpose for me. That’s what I’m saying to you. It’s okay to look to others for guidance. But eventually, you will need to discover your unique path.

Don’t settle for a watered-down version of yourself. You’ll only be limiting yourself. And you’ll undoubtedly be limiting what God can do through you. Who will represent you if you are busy trying to be a copycat of someone else? If two people are precisely the same, one of them will be unnecessary. Have you ever had duplicate files on your computer? Your computer will let you know so you can keep the original file and delete the copy to save space. Do you see the beauty and the importance of just being your authentic self? Never apologize to others for your uniqueness. Being different is a good thing. It means you have finally found the courage just to be yourself. God did not create you to blend in among the masses. He made you to stand out.

This means you can keep your eyes on heaven while your feet are firmly planted as you complete your earthly mission. God created you to be heavenly-minded, yet you have the potential to do earthly good because God endowed you with a plethora of gifts and talents to be used to impact the world. That uniqueness you have—the ingredient that sets you apart from the rest of humanity—is the key to your strength. It’s your superpower. Don’t run from your uniqueness; embrace it. Your uniqueness sets you apart from the rest. This is not by mistake—it’s divinely designed. To be authentic is to be right at home with yourself, being true to yourself and the godly values you represent.

Own Your Different

The life God has planned for you begins with owning your unique set of gifts, talents, and strengths. When you focus outwardly on the things others are doing, inwardly desiring the path they're on, you will become greatly confused and distracted. What does God's Word say about this? "Such a person is double-minded and unstable in all they do" (James 1:8 NIV). You don't have time for that. Instead, look to God and his Word for the validation you need.

As you pray for God's power, you'll be less tempted to seek the affirmation of others. Why? Because you won't need it. God's hand on your life is all the validation you need. God will continue to open doors for you as you do good because you only want to make him look good here on earth. Pattern your life after Christ. Look to him, He's where your true identity originates. You must never hesitate to embrace your true, authentic self. I'll remind you of what God told the prophet Samuel when he looked for Israel's next king. "Man looks at the outward appearance, but the Lord looks at the heart" (1 Samuel 16:7 NKJV).

Pause and Reflect

On a scale of 1 (none) to 5 (often), how frequently do you look to others to affirm the gifts you have? Are there any gifts you would use if you weren't concerned with what others might think? How do you think these gifts might line up with God's call on your life wherever you are serving now?

I'm approaching four decades in ministry since I retired from my job as a middle-high school music teacher. I found I didn't quit teaching. My classroom just got bigger. Take some advice from this classroom teacher. No matter how daunting the task may be, if God calls you to it, He will certainly empower you to do it. Remember, nobody can do what you can do like you can do it. Don't be afraid. Don't be intimidated. Be yourself. Everyone else is taken.

Leading in Prayer

Heavenly Father, thank you for making me not only different, but uniquely different. Help me remember you created me with gifts, talents, and strengths like no one else on the planet. Please give me the confidence to be the sole expression of myself. Not so I can look good, but so that I can give you glory with my life. Forgive me for looking to others and even the world for the validation I can only receive from you. As I read your Word, I will find my true identity in you. Amen.

"The world is going to decide who they think you are based on what you're portraying to them. You want them to know who you are so they won't have any surprises when you come out and live your life the way you're called to live it."

-Mandisa

Multi-Award-Gospel Recording Artist
& former "American Idol" Finalist

CHAPTER 26

Be a Surrendered Creative

Lisa Burris Burns

With more than 40 years of experience in the arts and 30+ years of platform ministry, Lisa Burris Burns thrives on the creative process. Always under the belief we can fine-tune our creative expression, she enjoys coaching up-and-coming artists. Her specialties include vocal and stage performance, public speaking and media writing, publicity, event planning, set design, and all things yarn and crafty.

Lisa lives in Blue Springs, Missouri, with her husband, Randy. The Burns have served in marriage and family ministry since 1988. They have six fantastic children, two amazing son-in-loves, and five adorable granddaughters. When Lisa isn't busy being a wife, mom, and Nonni, she enjoys the role of mentor and coach for KC Superstar. This four-month-long *American Idol*-style competition for area high school students serves as an annual fundraising event for "The JKC,"

the Jewish Community Center of Greater Kansas City. She has worked as a publicist and is an award-winning contributor to *Leading Hearts* magazine (leadinghearts.com). Her passion is to help people of all ages become the best version of themselves.

We're highly encouraged from a young age (some would say indoctrinated) to have a plan, be structured, and get after it. Success happens because we first do x-y-z. You know, set the goal, plot the journey, and see it through. Let's keep everything ordered and in sequence. Get the education, pay your dues, and climb our way to the top.

I spent my earliest days in a small rural farming community surrounded by both sides of my parent's families. There were cattle and Kansas wheat fields as far as you could see. I was the child who would strive to do my very best. Moving within well-plotted courses and constructs felt secure, predictable, and safe. Innately I loved to line things up and pay attention to the details. And yet, if I am being totally transparent, there were times situations felt a bit stifling. My mind loved everything in its place and ordered thinking, but it also swirled with ideas that felt like make-believe. Despite all my planned and ordered thoughts, I have a flair for the creative. To this day, I am often divided between logically and perfectly spaced ideals and possibilities that are birthed in daydreams and what-ifs. Stepping outside what was expected was a challenge and created inner tension. As the family's firstborn, hard-working and compliant, I tended to feel irresponsible when drawn into creative spontaneity. In a nutshell, I have often been torn between the strong desire to be ordered and structured, yet synchronously distracted by all things artistically flourished.

There are life experiences that cause me to say with confident excitement, Now this .... This all makes perfect, predictable, and logical sense. It's as it should be, given everything I've trained, worked toward, and planned. And then again, I have moments when I ask myself, How in the world did I arrive here? Seriously, who would have thought I'd be right here, doing this, right now? Certainly not me. I mean, I didn't plan for it, and it wasn't the neatly packaged outcome of forethought and set goals. My brain struggled to stretch wide enough to even consider most of the opportunities through which I've walked.

But that is my life—equal doses of what in the world and perfectly planned. It has taken time to embrace that an intentional Creator designed me to overflow with both. I've had to be willing to put aside my fears and insecurities. Accomplishing tasks with a brave heart and choosing a path in uncharted territory stretches you (often uncomfortably) to heights you didn't realize you could aspire. Knowing the Creator was thoughtful about my journey and how I am equipped for the space I'm in right now has made all the difference.

Pause and Reflect

In what ways are your childhood dreams and aspirations reflected in your daily life? Take time to list some of those dreams. Do you see any of your interests and talents in conflict with one another? If so, how has this affected your ability to focus over the years?

Embracing a Both/And Mentality

I must admit my willingness to embrace both sides—the administrative check-off-the-box girl and her free-spirited counterpart—was neither an easy nor an overnight journey. Many things influence us as we grow into our adult selves—our family, the community, and our culture.

For instance, music is at the core of my being. My parents graduated high school in the early '60s and had me before the age of 20. There was always music playing on the turntable or radio. Some of my favorite childhood memories include Daddy strumming a James Taylor song on his guitar. Momma would sing along with the radio and let me stay up late to watch a musical on television. By the time I was in middle school, my parents were working to provide me with vocal lessons. It made sense that music was something I would do. What sparked my interest as a child soon had me training, competing, and performing. I learned to live, eat, breathe, and excel in all things stage and song. Singing a thought-provoking lyric and melody was the place where all the daydreaming came to life. It sometimes felt like I was floating on a river current, just caught up with what was supposed to happen. My senior year began, and I did what seemed to be the right thing, the responsible thing, and auditioned for vocal scholarships at our state university. All the practice, planning, and passion for music paid off when I received a full ride to study voice. My next steps were falling into line.

I was walking in what appeared to be a perfect sequence of events, when I encountered a bend in the road ahead of me quite unexpectedly. I had a sweet friend who rode the bus to and from school with me daily. Her family had encountered Jesus over the summer, and there was no denying she was changed. From the minute she stepped on the bus that would take us to high school and the entire way home, she would share her journey. This went on for weeks.

Many people say we come into this world with a God-shaped hole or void that only He can fill. Deeper still, I believe we are intrinsically wired from our first moments of existence to connect with our Creator. While I wasn't raised attending weekly church services, I was keenly aware of his presence. I remember in grade school spending a Saturday night with my friend, Yvonne. My mom packed a dress so I could attend service with Yvonne's family at the local Lutheran church. I didn't understand all the words nor why there was the scent of burning incense, but I felt a strong sense of belonging. Throughout my childhood, I attended every church service anyone invited me to. Baptist Vacation Bible School? I went. Catholic mass? I was there for it. The local Charismatic Church youth meeting? Yes, please. The older I became, the more aware I was of God's presence. Those services moved me deeply, and I didn't know quite what to do with how they made me feel. Fast forward to my senior year of high school, and God allowed me to hear the redemption story through a teenage girl on a school bus. My life would never be the same, in the best way ever.

Looking back now at that turn in the road, I recognize it was the first of many times I would unexpectedly redirect. I also realize the One who knows and loves me best designed every bend in my path perfectly. When it happened, I wasn't sure how my future would turn out. I attended the university on a full vocal scholarship. One semester in, and much to my parent's demise, I walked away from the scholarship and transferred to a private Bible college. What was a nicely executed plan somehow turned sideways. On the one hand, I was full of apprehension and fear in the unknown. How would I pay for Bible college? Will my parents ever forgive me for giving up that scholarship? Is music still a part of the plan? On the other hand, I had tapped into a newfound sense of freedom. This feeling was all wrapped up in letting go. Letting go of my well-thought-out plans. Releasing the control I had over the outcome of those plans. Embracing the possibilities along the journey. Trusting in a God that slowly and surely was lighting up my world.

Pause and Reflect

How did the culture of your upbringing shape your adult aspirations? Take a moment to reflect on any detours you encountered along your life journey. How has your faith walk influenced the choices you have made? Describe a time when taking hold of a new opportunity involved letting go?

Mastering the Quick Change

As a new believer immersed in Bible college, my discipleship journey began in the classrooms of theologians. I learned to live up close and personal within the family of God—the girls living on my dorm floor. I learned to navigate and see the differences between performing versus service. I became increasingly aware of the presence of God and the sound of his whisper. Bible college is where I met my best friend, who I married a year and a half later. We didn't know where we were going, but we had each other and knew God was showing himself faithful.

The years carried us along as our sweet family grew with children. We embraced ministry together. Life was full and continued to get fuller. I was learning what it meant to become a mother, establish relationships, develop ministries, and etch out time to hear from God.

The more space that life consumed, the more I relied on easy tasks that didn't require me to work hard. Those made sense and were predictable. They were what I had trained for and I was confident I could do them. It felt good to contribute with the giftings I had. I continued to be the youth pastor's wife and a full-time mom. I sang with gospel groups, taught vocal lessons, and led worship. We moved several states away for Randy to study counseling and acquire his master's degree. With our third child on the way, I became the primary source of income by teaching at a local preschool. My husband went from stay-at-home dad/grad student by day to shift manager at Taco Bell by night. God was so good to us during those insanely blurred years.

Though I told myself it was only for a season, the days rolled into one another. Good memories alongside tragedy drove us to our knees and into each other's arms. We had an opportunity to move back home to be close to family. We lost a child and cared for loved ones who were struggling. Our family went from four to seven. As the children grew, so did our schedule, as we helped them acclimate. I was a master juggler, ever dancing in multiple directions. I continued leading worship weekly, sang in the choir, and started to coordinate all weddings and events for our very large congregation. I was consumed with the tasks of caregiving, doing what others needed or what I thought was expected of me. Most of the time, I ran on sheer adrenaline. Often when I needed to reach for the next thing, I did so on autopilot.

You have probably found yourself in the space of constant go, go, go. God has equipped many of us with the ability to multi-task profoundly. It truly is a superpower. When I commit to something, I'm all in—motherhood, production work, and service to others. However, if we're not careful, we can wake up one day not recognizing who we are or why we do what we do. For me, everything was about to come to a halt.

Pause and Reflect

How have the different roles you've played in life clouded or clarified your sense of purpose? What is your current understanding of God's purpose for your life? In what ways do you walk out your purpose in your day-to-day activity?

I wasn't feeling well. At 45, I found myself in a constant state of fatigue. I would push myself from one event to the next, and then my body would just stop. I would spend hours in continuous motion on a Sunday and then could barely make it up the stairs and into bed when I got home. The simplest daily household chores became difficult. I felt like I was trying to climb uphill in quicksand just showering, dressing, or brushing my teeth. Every muscle in my body felt like they were on fire, and my very bones ached. I realized this wasn't simply age or not being in the best of shape. I needed a physician.

The diagnosis was an autoimmune disease, and it looked like more than one. I was told that, short of a miracle, there was no cure. Medications and lifestyle changes could help with the extreme symptoms, but then again, they might not. Anything concerning my connective tissues (tendons, ligaments, and joints) was affected the most. Over a series of several weeks and multiple medical appointments, we had a plan of action but no quick and easy fix. If this was my new normal, I needed to get a feel for what it would take to improve my quality of life. I prayed God would heal me, knowing that he definitely could. I also prayed that if healing wasn't in the near future, he would somehow redeem these moments.

Everything about who I was and what seemed to make me, Lisa, was unsure. I didn't want to think about it. However, I realized the things I had become really good at—the daily dance of activity and even my vocal ability, were compromised. The conversation in my brain was ongoing, perhaps if I shift this around and only participate every other week? Maybe I lie low for a few days to conserve enough energy to marathon through this project? I eventually explained my situation to those with whom I served, worked and loved. I had a difficult time letting them down. Some relationships took a severe hit because I couldn't be on all the time. It is tough to understand and accept the limitations of a loved one with a chronic illness. I had to step away from certain commitments. I realized my focus needed to be on my family and doing what was necessary to regain my strength.

Those days were hard. To pull away from all I had busied myself with for so many years was painful. The music, specifically worship and platform ministry, had been a constant companion for 25 years. The connective tissue problems began to affect my singing voice. I can tell you now my identity was honestly quite shaken. My heart was hurting. In so many ways, I felt I didn't belong anymore and wasn't sure if I would ever belong again. A choice had to be made, and I was the only one who could make it. Was I going to stay stuck in my brokenness, or was I going to ask God to help me move forward?

Pause and Reflect

If you've experienced a life-altering event, how did it affect your sense of value and worth? How have you reconciled yourself to the loss you experienced due to that event? Are there any areas related to loss where you remain stuck?

A Risky Surrender

From the moment of diagnosis through those transitional years, and even now, my prayer became, "Jesus, I'm willing. I'm a willing participant in whatever you choose to do with me and through me. It doesn't have to be familiar. If you are with me, I say yes. It doesn't have to be predictable. I don't even have to feel like I can handle it. If you are with me, I will do it. I trust you." I didn't have a clue how God would take that little prayer and change everything, but He did. The bottom line, I had to readjust the expectations I had placed on myself. As I continued to learn more about my health and how to embrace my new way of doing life, I reminded God of my prayer. Along the way, I let my mind and heart wander again into daydreams and what-ifs.

A year later, when a friend asked, "Lisa, have you ever considered working in film?"

My response was to laugh and say absolutely, "No." She reminded me that having experience as a stage actor, I might really like it. But I couldn't picture it. I mean, I was a singer who couldn't sing consistently, and a stage play is so different from film work. I didn't know the first thing about filmmaking or auditioning for a movie. And yet, I couldn't quit thinking about the possibility that maybe God was putting feet on my I'm willing, and I say yes prayer. I returned to that friend, and with her help, I auditioned and landed a role in a feature-length film. I didn't sing one familiar note in that film. Nothing I had ever planned for or envisioned myself doing included me saying yes to a movie role.

Before I knew it, one opportunity bumped into the next. A random phone call came from another acquaintance asking if I might consider applying to work as a prop mistress for a movie-turned-stage play. She felt I could be the perfect fit, knowing my background. Once again, my immediate response was to reject the very thought. I mean, seriously, it was roughly a four-month commitment, almost four hours from my school-aged children and husband. How was this even possible? I remember almost laughing through my explanation of the call with my husband. It was a ridiculous idea, right? There was no way I was leaving all of them to go work with people I didn't really know. I would have to find a place to stay. My pay would have to outweigh what it would take to live there. Suddenly, the idea's absurdity came to a halt when Randy said, "I think this is a God thing, Lisa. I think you are supposed to do it. At the very least, listen to what they have to say." Hmmm, what was that prayer again?

Oh, that's right, I don't even have to feel like I can handle it. If you are with me, I will do it. I trust you.

Unbeknownst to me, every detail and concern I questioned was already covered. An old friend from high school connected me to a dear family that provided me a home away from home during the show's duration. They have become extended family to us, and we visit every chance we can. I'm sitting in the peace of their home on this day as I round out this chapter. One season of the show turned into two. I worked with some of the most gifted people who reinforced the power of true teamwork. With previous experience in front of an audience, I missed out on the brilliance of the movers and shakers behind the scenes. Their impact on me can't be measured. In my absence, my children and husband met every challenge without me just fine. The job ended up being such a sweet way for God to provide for and grow us all.

That out-of-town production experience coincided with my 16-year-old daughter winning a local singing competition. With time, I became a part of that incredible competition and the KC Superstar production team. Though heartache came with my chronic illness affecting my ability to perform, I've been able to pour what I know into others. For ten years, I've had the pleasure of coaching some of the most talented teen vocalists you will ever meet.

Before I knew it, women's magazines asked me to contribute by interviewing artists, authors, and film industry professionals. Once again, one opportunity leading to the next, I have had the honor of working as a publicist with the best, pitching some outstanding projects. Throw in a few more film and stage sets later, and I also said yes to set design and scripty duties. No, I didn't plan for any of it, but look what saying yes can do.

Pause and Reflect

Are you willing to allow God to use you in a way you haven't considered possible? Have you been presented with any opportunities that would enable you to reframe your gifts? List ways you have allowed your vision to be limited to what you are comfortable with and what you know.

Does He have Your Yes?

Ultimately, we have a choice to be willing participants in our life's story. Occasionally, my fears and insecurities have kept how I am used by God confined to a tiny space. We do come into this world with God-given abilities and passions. Certain events may leave us stumbling and surprised, but forward motion and redirection are possible. It doesn't have to look exactly as it has in the past. My own personal journey has taken flight into unchartered and gloriously new territories. God has strategically placed within you every detail that equips you for your right now journey with Jesus.

"Everything that goes into a life of pleasing God has been miraculously given to us by getting to know, personally and intimately, the One who invited us to God. The best invitation we ever received!" (2 Peter 1:3 The Message).

It isn't always predictable, comfortable, or without challenge. But when you add your own yes to the equation, you are on your way to quite the adventure.

Leading in Prayer

Heavenly Father, when my heart is torn between what makes sense and bold daydreams, I thank you for dwelling in the Both/And moments of my life. I ask you to guide me and continue to walk with me as I journey. Give me courage to take hold of opportunity as you lead me forward and beyond. While I love the comfort of familiar and predictable, let me embrace the adventure of unchartered territories ahead. I'm a willing participant and I trust you. If you are with me, I can do it. Amen.

"When I said yes to my first design project, and every time I've said yes since—showing up even though I wasn't an expert when I didn't know for sure if I could rise to the occasion—walking through each door is what led me to the next opportunity."

–Joanna Gaines

Co-Host of "Fixer Upper"
in *The Stories We Tell*

Lord,

Make me Your difference maker.
Where there is conflict,
Let me sow peace;
Where there is heartache, healing;
Where there is uncertainty, assurance;
Where there is disappointment, hope;
Where there are roadblocks, a better way;
Where there is worry, encouragement.
Heavenly Father,
Let me not strive to be served,
But to serve others in Your purpose,
Not seek to be honored as to give honor,
Rather than receive compassion to be compassionate.
For it is in blessing others that we are blessed,
It is in forgiving others that we are forgiven,
And it is in leading others in love that
We are empowered by the love of Christ.
Amen.

Linda Evans Shepherd (lindashepherd.com) is a best-selling prayer author and founder of the Advanced Writers And Speakers Association (awsa.com).

Acknowledgments

We are so blessed for the love and support of our project sisters including Cherie Denna, Lisa McIntire, Marilyn Luce Robertson, Jennifer Taylor, and Heather Van Allen, Andrea Tomassi, and interns Allyson Smyntek and Sarah Cummings. We couldn't have done this without you!

Made in the USA
Monee, IL
05 June 2023

35281895R00151